So you really want

Spanish

BOOK 1

Teacher's Book

So you really want to learn

Spanish

BOOK 1

Teacher's Book

Series Editor: Nicholas Oulton M.A. (Oxon.)

GALORE PARK

Published by Galore Park Publishing Ltd.,
PO Box 96, Cranbrook, Kent TN17 4WS

Text copyright © Galore Park 2003
Typography and layout by Typetechnique, London W1
Printed and bound by Ashford Colour Press

ISBN 1 902984 13 7

First published 2003

Also available:

Pupil's book	1902984102
Audio CD set	1902984250
Interactive CD Rom	1902984145

Acknowledgements

The publishers would like to thank the many generous people, without whose help the production of this book, and the CD that accompanies it, would have been impossible. In particular they would like to thank Cinta Romero for her tireless work in proof-reading and checking the answers to all the exercises. Special thanks are also due to:

Simon Craft, Elena de Celis, Ann Buxade del Tronco, Evelyne Shellard, Vanessa Fleitas Diaz, Janet Beloso, Peter Such, Keith Hannis, Alfredo Bello, Laura Vargas Llanas, Sara Foster, Maria Vidler, Maite Ross-Skedd, Carmen Brown, Andina Brown, Rosi Parker, Elena Peck, Miguel Alemany, Bella Griffith, Nick Griffith, Imanol Etxeberria, Tom and Alistair Davis, Richard Studholme, Tim Green, the "Spanish guitarist" at the Tone Zone Studio, Kevin Dodd, Emma Oulton, Sophie Oulton and Caterina Busquets.

CD Rom

The CD that accompanies this course was produced by Notes Re-Engineering Ltd. (www.evision.eu.com). The design and source code copyright is © Notes Re-Engineering Ltd 2003.

Contents

UNIT 1

About the unit

In this first unit pupils learn to ask and answer simple questions about themselves in Spanish. They learn some useful classroom phrases and vocabulary for classroom objects as well as basic rules of pronunciation and spelling.

Where the unit fits in

This is the first unit in a course for absolute beginners. It assumes no knowledge of MFL.

New language content:

- asking and responding to simple questions using *¿Cómo? ¿Cuándo? ¿Qué? ¿Cuánto?*
- introduction to verbs in first and second persons singular
- numbers 1–31
- rules and guidance for pronunciation and spelling
- definite and indefinite articles
- plurals of nouns
- use of *hay* and *no hay*

New contexts:

- meeting and greeting people, both formally and informally
- personal details (name, age, birthday)
- the alphabet
- months, dates, days of the week
- classroom objects
- classroom instructions

Expectations

At the end of this unit most pupils will: understand basic classroom instructions spoken by the teacher; greet people formally and informally; carry out short presentations about themselves using *y* and **pero**; hold simple conversations asking for information about others and giving information about themselves; identify and ask for classroom objects with correct indefinite article; make positive or negative responses to a request for an object; spell words, and ask for the meaning of the words they do not understand; use a dictionary to find the meaning or gender of a word they do not know; know how to pronounce words that follow a regular pattern.

Some pupils will not have made so much progress and will: understand the teacher's questions and instructions with some prompting or support; understand the words for classroom objects when they see and hear them; point to, and say the word for, a small number of everyday objects; be able to say a few phrases about themselves with the help of cue cards.

Some pupils will have progressed further and will: say and write longer passages from memory; use some classroom expressions independently and ask for help.

¡Hola y adiós!
Pupil's Book: Page 2; Audio track: 1

We begin the course with Juan, Cristina, José and Elena, giving the four greetings types for the different times of the day:

CD 1, track 1:

¡Hola!
¡Buenos días!
¡Buenas tardes!
¡Buenas noches!

Guidance on pronunciation is left until page 6 of the pupil's book.

Suggestion: At this stage, pupils should simply be encouraged to imitate what they hear. It is likely that some of them will comment on peculiarities such as the silent *h* in *hola,* the accent on *días* and the upside down punctuation.

Those using the CD Rom can click on each phrase to hear it pronounced individually.

¿Cómo te llamas?
Pupil's Book: Page 2; Audio track: 2

We then show how to introduce oneself correctly, using both the *tú* and the *usted* forms. Cristina is heard talking to Antonio, the school cook. Those using the CD Rom can watch a simple animation accompanied by speech bubbles containing the phrases as they are spoken.

CD 1, track 2:

¿Cómo te llamas?
Me llamo Cristina. ¿Cómo se llama usted?
Me llamo Antonio.

Tú and usted

Suggestion: Teachers may choose to give a very brief explanation of the difference between the *tú* and the *usted* forms at this stage, perhaps linking it to the *tu* and *vous* forms in French if appropriate. See also pupil's book p.32.

¿Qué tal?
Pupil's Book: Page 3; Audio track: 3

Pupils are now introduced to phrases for asking how one is, replying, and saying goodbye. Those using the CD Rom can watch a simple animation accompanied by speech bubbles containing the phrases as they are spoken.

CD 1, track 3:

¿Qué tal, Cristina?
Bien gracias. ¿Qué tal, Antonio?
Regular, gracias.
Adiós, Antonio.
Adiós, Cristina.

Exercise 1.1
Pupil's Book: Page 3; Audio tracks: 4 and 5

Before asking the pupils to practise the role-plays, two examples may be played, one for the familiar form (CD 1, track 4) and one for the polite form (CD 1, track 5).

CD 1, track 4:
(Ejemplo 1)

José:	*¡Hola!*
Cristina:	*¡Hola!*
José:	*¿Cómo te llamas?*
Cristina:	*Me llamo Cristina. Cómo te llamas?*
José:	*Me llamo José. ¿Qué tal Cristina?*
Cristina:	*Bien, gracias. ¿Qué hay, José?*
José:	*Regular, gracias. Adiós Cristina.*
Cristina:	*Hasta luego, José.*

CD 1, track 5:
(Ejemplo 2)

Antonio:	*¡Buenos días!*
Cristina:	*¡Buenos días!*
Antonio:	*¿Cómo te llamas?*
Cristina:	*Me llamo Cristina. ¿Cómo se llama usted?*
Antonio:	*Me llamo Antonio. ¿Qué tal, Cristina?*
Cristina:	*¡Fenomenal! gracias. Usted, Antonio, ¿Cómo está usted?*
Antonio:	*¡Fatal! ¡Fatal! Adiós Cristina.*
Cristina:	*¡Adiós Antonio!*

Suggestion: Pupils should be asked to comment on the difference between the familiar and polite forms, and to think of situations in English where we use different forms of address depending on who we are talking to.

Exercise 1.2
Pupil's Book: Page 3.

Those using the CD Rom can hear each phrase pronounced by clicking on it, and display the correct translations by clicking on the Union Flag icons.

1.   Hello!
2.   Good morning. What are you called?
3.   I am called Elena.
4.   Good morning. I am called Jorge. How are you?
5.   Hi. How are you?
6.   Well, thanks.
7.   Good afternoon. What are you called?
8.   Good afternoon. I am called Carolina. How are you?
9.   Okay thanks. How are you?
10. Brilliant, thanks. Goodbye.

Suggestion: Teachers may wish to highlight the difference between *muy bien* = very well and *muy buenas* = hi.

Vocabulario
Pupil's Book: Page 4

Regular learning of vocabulary is an important part of mastering a language. In each unit there are two main vocabularies for learning, and in addition there are frequent vocabulary boxes where a group of words is required to help with an exercise.

Suggestion: Pupils should be encouraged to keep their own vocabulary books, and to learn how to use the vocabularies at the back of the pupil's book.

Exercise 1.3
Pupil's Book: Page 4.

Either before or after pupils have practised this role-play, and written it out in Spanish, the suggested "answer" below may be discussed. Those using the CD Rom can watch a simple animation accompanied by speech bubbles containing these suggested phrases as they are spoken.

Miguel:	*Buenas tardes.*
Cristina:	*Buenas tardes.*
Miguel:	*Me llamo Miguel. ¿Cómo te llamas?*
Cristina:	*Me llamo Cristina.*
Miguel:	*¿Qué tal?*
Cristina:	*Bien, gracias. ¿Qué tal?*
Miguel:	*Fenomenal, gracias. Adiós.*
Cristina:	*Hasta la vista.*

Suggestion: Teachers may wish to stress that different phrases in Spanish have identical or similar meanings. For example *¿Qué tal?* and *¿Qué hay?*; *Hasta la vista* and *Hasta luego.* Pupils could think of examples of this in their own or any other language they know.

Los números 1-12
Pupil's Book: Page 4; Audio track: 6

The difficult *C* sounds in *cinco, once* and *doce*, the *CH* in *ocho* and the *Z* in *diez* may require particular attention, and some teachers may choose to skip forward to the sections on the alphabet and pronunciation on pages 6-7 of the pupil's book. Those using the CD Rom can hear each number pronounced individually by clicking on it. They may also see the similarities with the Latin numbers 1-12 by clicking on the **L** icon.

CD 1, track 6:

1, 2, 3, 4, 5, 6, 7, 8, 9, 10, 11, 12.

Exercise 1.4
Pupil's Book: Page 4; Audio track: 7

1. The first part of this exercise allows pupils using the CD Rom to hear a number of randomly generated numbers which they have to write down. The numbers that have been generated are recorded and may be displayed by clicking on "show number". (These numbers are different each time the exercise is run.) For those using the audio CD only, the numbers below are heard.

CD 1, track 7:

7, 1, 11, 3, 12, 10, 5, 6, 4, 8.

2. For pupils using the CD Rom, the second part of the exercise allows them to see a couple of dice rolling. They have to add the two numbers together and write down the total. Clicking on "throw" spins the dice; clicking on "answer" allows the sum of the two dice to be heard, accompanied by the caption "tengo x + y = z". Again, the numbers will be different each time the exercise is run.

For part two, pupils who are not using the CD Rom may roll their own dice or the teacher may write pairs of numbers on the board.

Exercise 1.5
Pupil's Book: Page 5.

For this exercise, pupils should be encouraged to work in pairs. One says the number, the other tries to write it down. They then change roles. Those using the CD Rom may hear the numbers by clicking on the red controller.

Suggestion: Particular care will be needed when differentiating the sounds for *seis* and *siete*, which are often confused by pupils in listening exercises.

Exercise 1.6
Pupil's Book: Page 5.

Pupils should say the sums to their partners, together with the answers. Those using the CD Rom may both see and hear the answers by clicking on the red **?** icons and red sound controllers respectively.

1.	*Dos más dos son cuatro*	$2 + 2 = 4$
2.	*Cuatro más uno son cinco*	$4 + 1 = 5$
3.	*Cinco más seis son once*	$5 + 6 = 11$
4.	*Ocho más cuatro son doce*	$8 + 4 = 12$
5.	*Seis más cuatro son diez*	$6 + 4 = 10$
6.	*Diez menos uno son nueve*	$10 - 1 = 9$
7.	*Nueve menos cuatro son cinco*	$9 - 4 = 5$
8.	*Ocho más dos son diez*	$8 + 2 = 10$
9.	*Doce menos cuatro son ocho*	$12 - 4 = 8$
10.	*Diez menos siete son tres*	$10 - 7 = 3$

Exercise 1.7
Pupil's Book: Page 5; Audio track: 8

In this exercise, the teacher puts a question to four pupils, Elena, Teresa, Ester and Pedro.

CD 1, track 8:

1.	*"Elena, ¿cuántos son dos más dos?"*	$2 + 2$
2.	*"Teresa, ¿cuántos son diez menos cinco?"*	$10 - 5$
3.	*"Ester, ¿cuántos son nueve menos dos menos siete?"*	$9 - 2 - 7$
4.	*"Pedro, ¿cuántos son uno más cinco más dos?"*	$1 + 5 + 2$

Pupils should write down the sums and the correct answers. Those using the CD Rom may both see and hear the answers by clicking on the red **?** icons and red sound controllers respectively.

Answers:

1.	Elena:	*"Dos más dos son cuatro."*	$2 + 2 = 4$
2.	Teresa:	*"Diez menos cinco son cinco."*	$10 - 5 = 5$
3.	Ester:	*"Nueve menos dos menos siete son cero."*	$9 - 2 - 7 = 0$
4.	Pedro:	*"Uno más cinco más dos son ocho."*	$1 + 5 + 2 = 8$

Exercise 1.8
Pupil's Book: Page 5.

In this exercise, pupils should practise their numbers by saying the sums and giving the answers. Those using the CD Rom may both see and hear the answers by clicking on the red **?** icons and red sound controllers respectively.

1.	*tres más cinco son ocho*	$3 + 5 = 8$
2.	*dos más uno son tres*	$2 + 1 = 3$
3.	*siete más cuatro son once*	$7 + 4 = 11$
4.	*cinco menos tres son dos*	$5 - 3 = 2$
5.	*diez menos uno son nueve*	$10 - 1 = 9$

Exercise 1.9
Pupil's Book: Page 5; CD 1, track 9

This game can be played at any stage, once the pupils have learnt sufficient numbers to play. A version of the game is available on the CD Rom which allows pupils to copy down the suggested Bingo card from the screen and then listen out for the numbers which are randomly generated each time the "call number" button is clicked. If pupils wish to hear a number repeated, clicking on "repeat number" will replay the last number called. When a line is complete (across, down or diagonally), pupils shout Bingo! After a short delay, the screen will flash, showing where the Bingo line was made. Clicking on "call number" at this stage will give the option of playing again. For those using the audio CD only, the following series of numbers is heard:

CD 1, track 9:

7, 3, 1, 2, 9, 4, 11, 6, 12, 8, 5, 10.

Pupils should make a card with nine numbers (chosen from 1-12) in rows of three, such as that shown below. When a row of **three** numbers is achieved (not four, as suggested in the book), be it across, down or diagonally, pupils should shout Bingo!

1	4	9
7	2	5
8	11	12

Suggestion: Pupils can be encouraged to take it in turns to be the bingo caller, with the rest of the class ticking off the numbers as they are called until a bingo line is achieved. Each number should only be called once in any one game. With only 12 numbers to play with, a bingo should be achieved quite quickly each time.

El alfabeto
Pupil's Book: Page 6; CD 1, track : 10

It is important to teach pupils the sound of the letters of the Spanish alphabet, which of course they will rarely (if ever) see written but which they will need to recognise and repeat, for example when spelling words out loud. By clicking on each letter of the alphabet on the CD Rom the name of the letter is pronounced aloud. Alternatively the whole alphabet may be heard by clicking on the red controller. Those using the CD Rom may hear examples of words using CH, LL and Ñ by clicking on the words in red.

CD 1, track 10:

A, B, C, CH, D, E, F, G, H, I, J, K, L, LL, M, N, Ñ, O, P, Q, R, S, T, U, V, W, X, Y, Z.

Los acentos
Pupil's Book: Page 6.

Many pupils will find the rules governing accents beyond them, and will pick up correct pronunciation simply by imitating their teacher. However the following examples (contained on the CD Rom) may be used to explain the basic principles. Clicking on each word allows it to be heard.

1. **Words ending in a vowel, *s* or *n*:**
   Stress **penultimate** syllable:
   España
   Barcelona
   Chile
   Inglaterra
   Torremolinos
   noches
   hablan

2. **All other words:**
   Stress **final** syllable:
   Madrid
   Benidorm
   curiosidad
   Miguel
   regular
   profesor

Exceptions to general rule:

Teachers may wish to give examples of words which break the rules learnt above, and which therefore receive an accent on the stressed syllable.

1. **Words ending in a vowel, *s* or *n*:**
   adiós
   jabón
   veintidós
   José

2. **All other words:**
   César
   lápiz
   imbécil
   Hernández
   Cristóbal

Suggestion: Although some pupils will find this lesson on accents difficult, they may find it a consolation to know that if a Spanish word has an accent, the word should always be stressed where the accent falls.

Exercise 1.10
Pupil's Book: Page 6; CD 1, track : 11

This exercise allows pupils to hear the ten words (listed in the pupil's book) pronounced, before they attempt to spell them back to their partners. Pupils should also be encouraged to try to write down these words as their partner or the teacher says them. They should not simply copy them from the book. Those using the CD Rom may either hear each word pronounced individually by clicking on the word, or the whole list of ten by clicking on the red controller.

CD 1, track 11:

España, Barcelona, Madrid, Inglaterra, Torremolinos, Costa Brava, Granada, Sevilla, Chile, Benidorm.

Exercise 1.11
Pupil's Book: Page 7; CD 1, tracks: 12-13

1. In the first part of this exercise, five pupils tell us their names, spell them out and say where they live.

CD 1, track 12:

Francisco: *Hola. Me llamo Francisco – F-r-a-n-c-i-s-c-o. Vivo en Sevilla – S-e-v-i-ll-a.*
Ester: *Hola. Me llamo Ester – E-s-t-e-r- y yo vivo en Ibiza – I-b-i-z-a.*
Rául : *Hola. Me llamo Rául – R-a con acento-u-l y yo vivo en Santillana – S-a-n-t-i-ll-a-n-a.*
Eduardo: *Buenos días, me llamo Eduardo – E-d-u-a-r-d-o. Vivo en Cádiz – C-a con acento – d-i-z.*
Cristina: *Buenas tardes. Me llamo Cristina – C-r-i-s-t-i-n-a y vivo en Granada – G-r-a-n-a-d-a.*

Answers:

Francisco vive en Sevilla.
Ester vive en Ibiza.
Rául vive en Santillana.
Eduardo vive en Cádiz.
Cristina vive en Granada.

Those using the CD Rom may click on the red **?** icons to reveal the answers in the table.

Suggestion: Teachers may wish to warn pupils to listen carefully for the *LL* letter in *Sevilla* and *Santillana*. Otherwise some may misspell these names.

Pupil's Book: Page 7; CD 1, track : 13

2. In the second part, the teacher is taking the register. The teacher calls out the names and pupils have to try to write down the names they hear.

CD 1, track 13:

Buenos días. Vamos a pasar lista. Manuel, Severiano, Juan, José, Pepe, Carolina, Ana, María, Teresa, Miguel.

Answers:

Manuel, Severiano, Juan, José, Pepe, Carolina, Ana, María, Teresa, Miguel.

Exercise 1.12
Pupil's Book: Page 7.

Pupils should be encouraged to practise spelling out their names to their partners. Pupils using the CD Rom can begin by clicking on the names listed on the screen in order to hear these names spelled out, letter by letter.

Pronunciation
Pupil's Book: Page 7.

Again, pronunciation will probably be learned gradually by imitation, but the basic rules should be covered and the following rules and examples will help. Pupils using the CD Rom can see the rules displayed on the screen; clicking on any of the Spanish words in italics (below) allows them to hear it pronounced.

1. **H** *¡Habla!*
2. **C + e, i** *Once, dieciséis.*
3. **G + e, i** *Geografía, Gibraltar.*
4. **J** *Jesús.*
5. **Z** *Cádiz.*
6. **B, V** *Baca, vaca.*
7. **R** *Ramón, Roberto.*
8. **RR** *Torremolinos.*
9. **Qu** *Quince.*

Exercise 1.13
Pupil's Book: Page 7.

This exercise allows pupils to link their understanding of the rules of pronunciation to a series of Spanish words. Pupils using the CD Rom can click on each word to hear it pronounced.

Suggestion: Linking words to the rules of pronunciation as listed in the pupil's book may not work for some pupils. However the exercise of pronouncing new words and thinking carefully about how they should be pronounced, particularly if they use any of the letters shown above, is extremely valuable in its own right.

¿Cuántos años tienes?
Pupil's Book: Page 8; CD 1, track : 14

Before pupils can practise giving their ages, the numbers up to 31 should be learned.

CD 1, track 14:

13, 14, 15, 16, 17, 18, 19, 20, 21, 22, 23, 24, 25, 26, 27, 28, 29, 30, 31.

Suggestion: Some teachers may wish to stress the similarities with French numbers at this stage. On the CD Rom the French numbers can be displayed or hidden, as the teacher wishes.

Exercise 1.14
Pupil's Book: Page 8.

In pairs, the pupils should ask how old they each are and say their own age.

Exercise 1.15
Pupil's Book: Page 8.
Answers:

1 + C
2 + E
3 + B
4 + A
5 + D

Those using the CD Rom may attempt to drag the correct answers (A-E) onto the corresponding questions (1-5). Selecting the wrong answer produces a discordant Spanish guitar sound!

Exercise 1.16
Pupil's Book: Page 9; CD 1, track : 15

In this listening exercise, the teacher calls out eight sums which the pupils have to calculate and write down. Pupils may choose to write all the sums down first and then work them out. Pupils using the CD Rom can click on the **?** icons to hear the sums and reveal the answers.

CD 1, track 15:

Número 1:   cinco multiplicado por cinco.
Número 2:   cuatro multiplicado por seis.
Número 3:   nueve multiplicado por tres.
Número 4:   diez dividido por dos.

Número 5:	*veintisiete dividido por tres.*
Número 6:	*veinte más nueve más dos.*
Número 7:	*veintiocho menos cuatro.*
Número 8:	*cinco multiplicado por dos.*

Answers:

1.	5 x 5 = 25		5.	27 ÷ 3 = 9
2.	4 x 6 = 24		6.	20 + 9 + 2 = 31
3.	9 x 3 = 27		7.	28 – 4 =24
4.	10 ÷ 2 = 5		8.	5 x 2 = 10

Exercise 1.17
Pupil's Book: Page 9; CD 1, track : 16

In this listening exercise, pupils hear a number of characters introducing themselves and their friends and giving their ages. Where pupils are filling in the table with complete sentences, as in the example, care should be taken over the plural form *tienen* required for Miguel and Rafael; the more able pupils will have noticed it in the rubric to the exercise (*¿Cuántos años tienen?*).

CD 1, track 16:

José:	*Hola. Me llamo **José**. Tengo once años.*
María:	*Buenos días. Me llamo **María**. Tengo doce años.*
Jesús:	*Buenas noches. Mi nombre es **Jesús**. Tengo dieciséis años.*
	*Hola. Te presento a mi amigo **Juan**, que tiene diecinueve años.*
	*Aquí está **Teresa**. Teresa tiene quince años.*
	*Aquí están **Miguel y Rafael**. Tienen dieciséis años.*
	*Te presento a mi amiga **Carmen**, que tendrá quince años el año que viene.*
	*Aquí está **Pedro**. Mañana Pedro tendrá veintidós años.*

Answers:

José tiene 11 años.
María tiene 12 años.
Jesús tiene 16 años.
Juan tiene 19 años.
Teresa tiene 15 años.
Miguel y Rafael tienen 16 años.
Carmen tiene 14 años.
Pedro tiene 21 años.

Pupils using the CD Rom can click on the **?** icons to reveal the answers.

Suggestion: Pupils will need to have set out the table before the track is played, so that they need only listen out for the ages and note these down. Teachers may choose to point out the future form (*tendrá*) encountered in the last two sections, and to emphasise that it is the age *today* of these pupils that we wish to know, not what age they will be in the future; alternatively they may wish to see which of their pupils spots the "trap" and is able to adjust their answers accordingly. The phrases *el año que viene* and *mañana* should be sufficient signposts for most.

Exercise 1.18
Pupil's Book: Page 9; CD 1, track : 17

In this exercise, pupils have to identify which number has been left out of the sequence.

CD 1, track 17:

1. *Once, doce, trece, quince*
2. *Veinticuatro, veintiséis, veintisiete, veintiocho*
3. *Trece, catorce, dieciséis, diecisiete*
4. *Seis, ocho, nueve, diez*
5. *Veintisiete, veintiocho, treinta, treinta y uno*
6. *Diecinueve, veintiuno, veintidós, veintitrés*

Answers (missing numbers shown in bold):

1. *Once, doce, trece, **catorce**, quince*
2. *Veinticuatro, **veinticinco**, veintiséis, veintisiete, veintiocho*
3. *Trece, catorce, **quince**, dieciséis, diecisiete*
4. *Seis, **siete**, ocho, nueve, diez*
5. *Veintisiete, veintiocho, **veintinueve**, treinta, treinta y uno*
6. *Diecinueve, **veinte**, veintiuno, veintidós, veintitrés*

Pupils using the CD Rom can click on the **?** icons to reveal the answers.

Exercise 1.19
Pupil's Book: Page 9.

In this exercise another game of bingo may be played. Pupils should copy one or more of the three cards, as shown in the pupil's book, and try to work out who wins the game, José, Rafael or Carolina. The winner is the one who gets a row of four numbers in a straight line (including diagonal). Pupils may decide to select just one of the three characters, and listen out only for the numbers on that character's card. More able pupils may prefer to listen out to all the numbers and tick them off on the appropriate cards as they occur. The numbers read out are shown below.

CD 1, track 18:

5, 14, 12, 2, 18, 3, 7, 22, 20, 1, 29, 30, 19, 27.

Pupils using the CD Rom may play the game on the screen by clicking on "call number", in which case the numbers are generated afresh each time the game is played.

Los meses y las estaciones del año
Pupil's Book: Page 10; CD 1, track : 19

CD 1, track 19:

enero, febrero, marzo, abril, mayo, junio, julio, agosto, septiembre, octubre, noviembre, diciembre.

Suggestion: Pupils should be warned not to use capital letters for the months, as they do in English.

Exercise 1.20
Pupil's Book: Page 10; Screen 57; CD 1, track : 20

CD 1, track 20:

1. *Los españoles celebran el día de la Hispanidad el 12 de octubre.*
2. *En Valencia se celebran las fallas el 19 de marzo.*
3. *San Isidro tiene lugar del 8 al 15 de mayo.*
4. *El 1 de noviembre es el día de Todos los Santos.*
5. *Se celebra San Juan el 24 de junio.*
6. *Se celebra la Tomatina en Buñol, el último miércoles de cada agosto – empieza a las 11 en punto.*
7. *La Tamborrada tiene lugar del 19 hasta el 20 de enero.*
8. *Las fiestas de las Navidades empiezan el 24 de diciembre y terminan el 6 de enero.*
9. *Se celebra El día de los Reyes el 6 de enero.*
10. *Se celebra San Fermín del 6 hasta el 14 de julio.*
11. *Se celebran Las Nieves de Pontevedra el 29 de julio.*
12. *Suele celebrarse La Feria de Abril al fin de abril (depende de la fecha de la Semana Santa).*

Translation:

1. The Spanish celebrate *el día de la Hispanidad* on 12th October.
2. In Valencia they celebrate *las fallas* on 19th March.
3. *San Isidro* lasts from 8th-15th May.
4. 1st November is the day of *Todos los Santos* (All Saints Day).
5. *San Juan* is celebrated on 24th June.
6. *La Tomatina* is celebrated in Bunol, Valencia, on the last Wednesday of every August – it begins at 11 o'clock exactly.
7. *La Tamborrada* takes place on January 19th till 20th.
8. *La Navidad* takes place from December 24th to January 6th.
9. *El día de Reyes* is celebrated on 6th January.
10. *San Fermín* is celebrated from 6th – 14th July.
11. *Las Nieves Pontevedra* takes place on July 29th.
12. *La Feria de Abril* normally takes place at the end of April (it depends when Easter is).

Answers:

1.	*El día de la Hispanidad*	*12 de octubre.*
2.	*Las fallas de Valencia*	*19 de marzo.*
3.	*San Isidro*	*8 – 15 de mayo.*
4.	*Todos los Santos.*	*1 de noviembre.*
5.	*San Juan*	*24 de junio.*
6.	*La Tomatina*	*el último miércoles de agosto.*
7.	*La Tamborrada*	*19 – 20 de enero.*
8.	*Navidad*	*24 de diciembre – 6 de enero.*
9.	*El día de los Reyes*	*6 de enero.*
10.	*San Fermín*	*6 – 14 de julio.*
11.	*Las Nieves Pontevedra*	*29 de julio.*
12.	*La Feria de Abril*	*al fin de abril (depende de la Semana Santa).*

Pupils using the CD Rom can see photographs for each festival and hear the description by clicking on the names. Clicking on the **?** icons reveals the answers.

Exercise 1.21
Pupil's Book: Page 11.

This exercise provides practise at giving dates. Pupils will almost certainly have to research many of these dates before they can put them into Spanish. This gives teachers an opportunity to highlight similarities and differences between key dates in the two countries.

1.	Christmas Eve	24th December
2.	Christmas Day	25th December
3.	Boxing Day	26th December (not celebrated in Spain)
4.	New Years Eve	31st December
5.	New Year's Day	1st January
6.	Your birthday	? (pupils supply own birthdays)
7.	St. Valentines Day	14th February
8.	St. George's Day	23rd April
9.	St. Andrew's Day	30th November
10.	St. Patrick's Day	17th March
11.	St. David's Day	1st March
12.	Midsummer's Day	23rd or 24th June (San Juan)

Those using the CD Rom can display the correct dates by clicking on the red **?** icons, and can hear the suggested answers (below) by clicking on the audio icons on the left of the screen.

Suggested answers:

1. *La Nochebuena se celebra el 24 de diciembre.*
2. *El día de Navidad se celebra el 25 de diciembre.*
3. *"Boxing Day", el 26 de diciembre, no se celebra en España.*
4. *La Nochevieja se celebra el 31 de diciembre.*
5. *El día del Año Nuevo se celebra el primero de enero.*
6. *Mi cumpleaños es el ...*
7. *El día de St. Valentine se celebra el 14 de febrero.*
8. *El día de St. George se celebra el 23 de abril.*
9. *El día de St. Andrew se celebra el 30 de noviembre.*
10. *El día de St. Patrick Day se celebra el 17 de marzo.*
11. *El día de St. David se celebra el primero de marzo.*
12. *"Midsummer's Day," (en españa "la Fiesta de San Juan"), se celebra el 23 o 24 de junio.*

¿Cuándo es tu cumpleaños?
Pupil's Book: Page 11.

Those using the CD Rom may listen to the examples by clicking on the controller buttons on the screen.

Exercise 1.22
Pupil's Book: Page 11.

In this exercise, the pupils should take turns to ask when their friends' birthdays are and how old they are. The polite form should be used if they address an adult. Those using the CD Rom can watch a simple animation by clicking on the **start** button on their screens and then **play** on the red controller.

Profesora: *¿Cuándo es tu cumpleaños y cuántos años tienes?*
Elena: *Mi cumpleaños es el 27 de noviembre y tengo quince años.*
¿Cuándo es su cumpleaños y cuántos años tiene?
Profesora: *Mi cumpleaños es el 23 de febrero y tengo treinta años.*

Exercise 1.23
Pupil's Book: Page 11; CD 1, track : 21

In this exercise, six characters introduce themselves and give their birthdays.

CD 1, track 21:

1.	**Manuel:**	*¡Hola! Me llamo Manuel. Mi cumpleaños es el 13 de mayo.*
2.	**Severiano:**	*¡Hola! Me llamo Severiano. Mi cumpleaños es el 3 de junio.*
3.	**Juan:**	*Buenos días. Me llamo Juan y mi cumpleaños es el 22 de julio.*
4.	**José:**	*Buenas tardes. Me llamo José y mi cumpleaños es el 2 de septiembre.*
5.	**Pepe:**	*Me llamo Pepe. Mi cumpleaños es el 17 de enero.*
6.	**Carolina:**	*Hola. Me llamo Carolina. Mi cumpleaños es el 23 de febrero.*

Answers:

1.	*Manuel*	*13 de mayo*
2.	*Severiano*	*3 de junio*
3.	*Juan*	*22 de julio*
4.	*José*	*2 de septiembre*
5.	*Pepe*	*17 de enero*
6.	*Carolina*	*23 de febrero*

Pupils using the CD Rom can click on the red controllers to play the sound files and the **?** icons to reveal the answers.

Exercise 1.24
Pupil's Book: Page 11; CD 1, track : 22

In this exercise, the six characters give their ages.

CD 1, track 22:

1.	**Profesora:**	*Manuel, ¿cuántos años tienes?*
	Manuel:	*Tengo 12 años.*
2.	**Profesora:**	*Severiano, ¿cuántos años tienes?*
	Severiano:	*Tengo 13 años.*
3.	**Profesora:**	*Juan, ¿cuántos años tienes?*
	Juan:	*Tengo 16 años.*
4.	**Profesora:**	*José, ¿cuántos años tienes?*
	José:	*Mi cumpleaños es el 2 de septiembre y tengo 15 años.*
5.	**Profesora:**	*Pepe, ¿cuántos años tienes?*
	Pepe:	*Tengo 5 años! No ¡es broma! Tengo 15 años.*
6.	**Pepe:**	*Carolina, ¿cuántos años tienes?*
	Profesora:	*Treinta, yo tengo treinta años. Mi cumpleaños es el 23 de febrero.*

Answers:

1.	*Manuel*	*12*
2.	*Severiano*	*13*
3.	*Juan*	*16*
4.	*José*	*15*
5.	*Pepe*	*15*
6.	*Profesora*	*30*

Pupils using the CD Rom can click on the red controllers to play the sound files and the **?** icons to reveal the answers.

Suggestion: Teachers may wish to comment on the fact that Pepe addresses his teacher by her first name, a common practice in Spain.

Exercise 1.25
Pupil's Book: Page 12; CD 1, track : 23

In this exercise five characters introduce themselves, say where they live, give their age and tell us when their birthdays are.

CD 1, track 23:

María: *"Hola. Me llamo María y vivo en Barcelona. Tengo 15 años y mi cumpleaños es el 22 de febrero."*

Sergio: *"Buenos días. Me llamo Sergio y vivo en Toledo. Tengo 19 años y mi cumpleaños es el 30 de Julio."*

David: *"Hola. Me llamo David. Vivo en Badajoz y mi cumpleaños es el 12 de marzo. Tengo 14 años."*

Ana: *"Hola. Me llamo Ana y tengo 18 años. Mi cumpleaños es el 17 de mayo. Vivo en Cádiz."*

Miguel: *"Buenos días. Me llamo Miguel y vivo en Mallorca. ¡Hoy cumplo 23 años!"*

Answers:

	Nombre	Ciudad	Edad	Cumpleaños
1.	María	Barcelona	15	22 de febrero
2.	Sergio	Toledo	19	30 de julio
3.	David	Badajoz	14	12 de marzo
4.	Ana	Cádiz	18	17 de mayo
5.	Miguel	Mallorca	23	Today's date

Suggestion: Pupils should have prepared the table before they begin listening to the audio tracks.

Pupils using the CD Rom can click on the red controllers to play the sound files and the **?** icons to reveal the answers.

Los días de la semana
Pupil's Book: Page 12.

Those using the CD Rom can click on each day to hear it pronounced.

Exercise 1.26
Pupil's Book: Page 12.

This exercise allows pupils to practise posing and responding to questions about the date. The past tense after *ayer* should be pointed out.

Those using the CD Rom can click on the audio buttons on the screen to hear the current date, tomorrow's date and yesterday's date. These are controlled by the computer's system clock and update on a daily basis. In addition, a suggested response to question 9 is given as follows:

Pues...¡Es el 25 de diciembre! ¿Y el tuyo?

Exercise 1.27
Pupil's Book: Page 12.

A possible conversation, based on the four pictures, is given below, and may be heard by those using the CD Rom. Any prompts could be used here, but the general topics covered so far (greetings, introductions, state of welfare, birthdays, dates and farewells) need to be practised until they come naturally.

José:	*"¡Hola!"*
Cristina:	*"¡Hola!"*
José:	*"¿Cómo te llamas?"*
Cristina:	*"Me llamo Cristina. ¿Cómo te llamas?"*
José:	*"Me llamo José. ¿Qué tal, Cristina?"*
Cristina:	*"Bien, gracias. Y tu, ¿qué hay, José?"*
José:	*"Regular, gracias."*
Cristina:	*"¿Cuándo es su cumpleaños?"*
José:	*"Mi cumpleaños es es el 2 de septiembre."*
Cristina:	*"¿Cuál es tu fiesta favorita?"*
José:	*"Mi fiesta favorita es...pues – las fallas de Valencia. Adiós, Cristina."*
Cristina:	*"Adiós, José."*

Vocabulario 1.1
Pupil's Book: Page 13.

Learning vocabulary is too often neglected, often due to time constraints. This *vocabulario* box is one of twelve in the book and may be used to emphasise vocabulary as a learning objective in its own right.

La clase
Pupil's Book: Page 14.

Those using the CD Rom may click on each item to hear it pronounced.

Nouns and gender

Pupils should be taught the basic guidelines for establishing the gender of a noun:

- The vast majority of words which end in *-o* are masculine.
- The vast majority of words which end in *-a* are feminine.
- All words that end in *-dad* or *-ción* are feminine.

Examples of masculine nouns in *-o*:

el bolígrafo	= the pen
el cuaderno	= the exercise book
el libro	= the book
el rotulador	= the board-marker

Examples of feminine nouns in *-a*:

la goma	= the rubber
la mesa	= the table
la pizarra	= the whiteboard
la silla	= the chair

Examples of feminine nouns in *-dad* and *-ción*:

la calidad	= the quality	*la canción*	= the song
la cantidad	= the quantity	*la estación*	= the station, season
la ciudad	= the city	*la evaluación*	= the assessment
la edad	= the age	*la habitación*	= the room

These examples may be displayed on the screen by those using the CD Rom by clicking on the red **?** buttons beside each of the three rules.

Definite and indefinite articles
Pupil's Book: Page 15.

Both definite and indefinite articles are introduced at this stage as it is considered that to force the use of one article where the other is more natural would lead to bad habits. Those using the CD Rom may click on each example (as set out in the pupil's book) to hear it pronounced.

Exercise 1.28
Pupil's Book: Page 15.

This exercise gives pupils practice at using the phrases *¿dónde está?* and *aquí está*. Those using the CD Rom can watch a simple animation with the following sound track:

Carolina:	*¿Dónde está el cuaderno?*
José:	*Aquí está el cuaderno.*
Carolina:	*¿Dónde está el bolígrafo?*
José:	*Aquí está el bolígrafo.*

Exercise 1.29
Pupil's Book: Page 16; CD 1, track : 24

This simple reading passage may be listened to on the CD before pupils translate it into English. Alternatively the exercise may be run as a pure listening exercise, with the teacher asking questions such as the following:

1. What is the name of the boy?
2. What is the name of the girl?
3. Which three items does the girl ask for?
4. Where is the 3rd item?

CD 1, track 24:

Rosa:	*Buenos días, José.*
José:	*Buenos días, Rosa.*
Rosa:	*¿Dónde está el bolígrafo?*
José:	*Aquí está el bolígrafo.*
Rosa:	*¿Dónde está el libro?*
José:	*Aquí está el libro.*
Rosa:	*¿Dónde está el rotulador?*
José:	*Aquí está, en la mesa.*

Those using the CD Rom may click on the red controller to hear the passage read aloud. Clicking on the Union Flag icon reveals the English translation:

Good morning, José.
Good morning, Rosa.

Where is the pen?
Here is the pen.
Where is the book?
Here is the book.
Where is the board marker?
Here it is, on the table.

Suggestion: This may be a good time to point out that Spanish uses the same word for "in" and "on".

Exercise 1.30
Pupil's Book: Page 16.

Conversations will at this stage necessarily be extremely limited, but the pictures give prompts for some of the simple topics covered so far, even if the result is no more than a series of questions and answers using *¿Dónde está* and *Aquí está*.

E.g. Picture 1:   *¿Dónde está el profesor?*
                    Aquí está el profesor.

Singular and plural
Pupil's Book: Page 17.

Those using the CD Rom may click on the words to hear them pronounced in both the singular and plural. Teachers may wish to add that nouns ending in *s* (e.g. *sacapuntas*) do not change in the plural. E.g. *El sacapuntas, los sacapuntas.*

Exercise 1.31
Pupil's Book: Page 17.
Answers:

1.   *Un libro*
2.   *Unos libros*
3.   *Una mesa*
4.   *Unas mesas*
5.   *El cuaderno*
6.   *Los cuadernos*
7.   *Una goma*
8.   *Unas gomas*
9.   *Una silla*
10. *Unas sillas*

Those using the CD Rom may click on the Spanish flag icon to reveal the translations.

Exercise 1.32
Pupil's Book: Page 17.
Suggested answers:

1.   *una mesa, cuatro sillas y unas flores.*
2.   *tres sacapuntas* y un cuaderno.*
3.   *dos gomas y cuatro reglas.*
4.   *nueve bolígrafos y un lápiz.*
5.   *una pizarra, siete sillas, un pupitre, un profesor y dos chicas.*

*Pupils should be told that the few Spanish nouns ending in *s* do not generally change in the plural. Those using the CD Rom may click on the Spanish flag icons to reveal the answers.

Exercise 1.33
Pupil's Book: Page 18.

	Singular	Plural	Translation
1.	El año	Los años	The years
2.	Un chico	Unos chicos	Some boys
3.	La clase	Las clases	The classes
4.	Un acento	Unos acentos	Some accents
5.	El número	Los números	The numbers
6.	Una silla	Unas sillas	Some chairs
7.	La profesora	Las profesoras	The teachers
8.	Una mesa	Unas mesas	Some tables
9.	El nombre	Los nombres	The names
10.	La regla	Las reglas	The rulers

Those using the CD Rom may click on the red ? icons to reveal the plurals and the Union Flag icons to reveal the translations.

Por favor
Pupil's Book: Page 18.

Those using the CD Rom may watch a simple animation to illustrate the use of *por favor*, as follows:

José: *Elena, ¿tienes un lápiz, por favor?*
Elena, do you have a pencil, please?

Elena: *No. No tengo un lápiz.*
No. I don't have a pencil.

José: *Juan, por favor....*
Juan, please...

Juan: *¡No! No tengo un lápiz.*
No. I don't have a pencil.

José: *Por favor, profesor. ¿Usted tiene un lápiz?*
Please, sir. Do you have a pencil?

Profesor: *Sí, aquí está* un lápiz.*
Yes, here's a pencil.

José: *Gracias.*
Thank you.

***N.B**. The use of *hay* is introduced on page 20 of the pupil's book.

Exercise 1.34
Pupil's Book: Page 18; CD 1, track : 25.

In this exercise, pupils listen to four dialogues and then mark the statements below as true or false.

CD 1, track 25:

Carolina: *José, ¿tienes un rotulador, por favor?*

José: *Sí, tengo.*

Carolina: *¿Tienes una regla?*

José: *Lo siento, no tengo una regla.*

Carolina:	*Miguel, ¿tienes tu libro de español?*
Miguel:	*Lo siento, no tengo.*
Carolina:	*¿Tienes tu cuaderno?*
Miguel:	*Sí, aquí está.*
Elena:	*Ana, ¿tienes un bolígrafo, por favor?*
Ana:	*Lo siento, no lo tengo.*
Elena:	*¿Tienes una goma?*
Ana:	*Si, la tengo. Toma.*
Elena:	*Gracias.*
Ana:	*De nada.*
Ana:	*María, ¿tienes un lapiz, por favor?*
María:	*Sí, tengo dos lápices. Toma uno.*
Ana:	*Gracias.*
María:	*De nada.*
Ana:	*¿Tienes un sacapuntas?*
María:	*Lo siento, no tengo.*

Translations:

Carolina:	José, do you have a board marker, please?
José:	Yes, I have one.
Carolina:	Do you have a ruler?
José:	Sorry, I don't have a ruler.
Carolina:	Miguel, do you have your Spanish book?
Miguel:	Sorry, I don't have it.
Carolina:	Do you have a textbook?
Miguel:	Yes, here it is.
Elena:	Ana, do you have a pen, please?
Ana:	Sorry, no I don't.
Elena:	Do you have a rubber?
Ana:	Yes I do. Here you are.
Elena:	Thanks.
Ana:	Not at all.
Ana:	María, do you have a pencil, please?
María:	Yes, I have two pencils. Take one.
Ana:	Thanks.
María:	Not at all.
Ana:	Do you have a pencil-sharpener?
María:	Sorry, no I don't.

Answers:

1.	*José tiene un rotulador.*	*Verdad*
2.	*José no tiene una regla.*	*Verdad*
3.	*Miguel tiene un libro de español.*	*Mentira*
4.	*Miguel no tiene un cuaderno.*	*Mentira*
5.	*Ana tiene un bolígrafo.*	*Mentira*
6.	*Ana no tiene una goma.*	*Mentira*
7.	*María tiene un lápiz.*	*Verdad*
8.	*María no tiene un sacapuntas.*	*Verdad*

Those using the CD Rom may click on the red **?** icons to reveal the answers (true or false).

Exercise 1.35
Pupil's Book: Page 18.

Pupils should now have little difficulty talking about basic classroom objects using *¿Tienes...?* and *Tengo*. Those using the CD Rom may view a number of items to ask about.

Exercise. 1.36
Pupil's Book: Page 19; CD 1, track : 26

In this exercise, which may be read and/or listened to, the teacher asks a number of pupils about a range of classroom objects which they should have with them. Eduardo is found to be somewhat lacking in this department.

CD 1, track 26:

Profesora:	*Buenos días, chicos.*
Alumnos:	*Buenos días, señorita.*
Profesora:	*José, ¿qué tienes en tu mochila? ¿Tienes tus libros?*
José:	*Sí, señorita. Tengo tres libros en mi mochila. Tengo mi libro de español, mi libro de inglés y mi cuaderno.*
Profesora:	*Bien. Y tú, Teresa, ¿tienes tus libros?*
Teresa:	*Sí. Pero no tengo mi libro de historia.*
Profesora:	*¿Dónde está?*
Teresa:	*Está en casa. Está en la mesa en casa. Lo siento.*
Profesora:	*No importa. Eduardo, ¿tienes tus libros?*
Eduardo:	*No, señorita. Mis libros están en casa.*
Profesora:	*¿Tienes tu bolígrafo?*
Eduardo:	*¡No, mi bolígrafo está en el autobús!*
Profesora:	*No tienes tus libros ni tu bolígrafo, pero tienes tu regla, ¿verdad?*
Eduardo:	*No, señorita. Creo que Teresa tiene mi regla.*
Teresa:	*¡Qué va! No tengo su regla.*
Eduardo:	*¡Qué sí!*
Teresa:	*¡Qué no! Eduardo es imbécil!*
Profesora:	*¡Oye! ¡Basta! Eduardo, ¿tienes tu calculadora?*
Eduardo:	*Sí, claro.*

Profesora:	*¿Dónde está tu calculadora?*
Eduardo:	*Está en mi mochila, claro.*
Profesora:	*¿Estás seguro?*
Eduardo:	*Sí, aquí está ... ¡Ay!, no tengo mi calculadora. Quizás Teresa ...*
Teresa:	*¡Qué va! Eduardo es ....*
Profesora:	*¡Basta!*

Translation:

Profesora:	Good morning, guys.
Alumnos:	Good morning, miss.
Profesora:	José, what do you have in your schoolbag? Do you have your books?
Jose:	Yes, miss. I have three books in my school bag. I have my Spanish book, my English book and my exercise book.
Profesora:	Good. And you, Teresa, do you have your books?
Teresa:	Yes. But I don't have my History book.
Profesora:	Where is it?
Teresa:	It's at home. It's on the table at home. I'm sorry.
Profesora:	Don't worry. Eduardo, do you have your books?
Eduardo:	No, miss. My books are at home.
Profesora:	Do you have your pen?
Eduardo:	No, my pen is on the bus.
Profesora:	You don't have your books or your pen, but you have your ruler, don't you?
Eduardo:	No, miss. I think that Teresa has my ruler.
Teresa:	No way! I don't have his ruler.
Eduardo:	Yes you do!
Teresa:	No I don't! Eduardo is stupid!
Profesora:	Hey, that's enough! Eduardo, do you have your calculator?
Eduardo:	Yes, of course.
Profesora:	Where is your calculator?
Eduardo:	It's in my school bag, of course.
Profesora:	You're sure?
Eduardo:	Yes, here it is...Oh, I don't have my calculator. Perhaps Teresa...
Teresa:	No way! Eduardo is...
Profesora:	Enough!

Answers:

1. *Teresa no tiene su **libro de historia**.*
2. *Su libro de historia está **en la mesa** en casa.*
3. *El bolígrafo de Eduardo está **en el autobús**.*
4. *Eduardo no tiene sus **libros** ni su **bolígrafo** ni su **regla** ni su **calculadora**.*
5. *Eduardo cree que **Teresa** tiene su calculadora.*

Those using the CD Rom may click on the red **?** icons to reveal the answers.

Exercise 1.37
Pupil's Book: Page 20.

In this exercise, pupils should practise asking and answering the question *¿Qué es esto?* using the pictures in the book as a prompt. Those using the CD Rom may click on the Spanish flag icons to reveal (and hear) the following answers:

1. *Es un diccionario.*
2. *Son unas tijeras.*
3. *Es un pupitre.*
4. *Es un ordenador.*
5. *Es un mapa.*
6. *Es una ventana.*
7. *Es una carpeta.*
8. *Es una puerta.*
9. *Es una luz.*
10. *Es un tablón.*

En mi mochila tengo
Pupil's Book: Page 20.

This exercise is very good for practising vocabulary and is a version of the game "I packed my Saratoga trunk and in it I put…" Pupils take it in turns to add an item and have to remember each of the items added so far, in the correct sequence. Those using the CD Rom may click on the "show individually" button to reveal a series of pictures (which they have to identify and add to their school bag), and the "show all" button to show all the pictures together.

Hay
Pupil's Book: Page 20.

Those using the CD Rom may display the information on *hay* on the screen, and click on the phrases to hear them pronounced.

Suggestion: Some pupils may need reminding that the initial *h* of *hay* is silent.

Exercise 1.38
Pupil's Book: Page 20.

Another opportunity for pupils to practise what they have learnt so far in pairs or groups.

Los imperativos
Pupil's Book: Page 21.

Those using the CD Rom may display the information on imperatives and hear each of the examples pronounced.

Suggestion: Pupils need to be aware that a singular imperative is one in which a person or persons is giving a command **to one person**; a plural imperative is one in which a person or persons is giving a command **to more than one person**. Many pupils find this confusing, thinking that the number of people **giving the command** is the relevant factor.

Simon dice
Pupil's Book: Page 21; CD 1, track : 27

A simple way to practise imperatives is to play "Simon says". Pupils listen to a series of instructions but should only follow the instructions if they hear the phrase *Simon dice*.

CD 1, track 27:

Simon dice: ¡sentaos!	Simon says: sit down!
Simon dice: ¡mirad la pizarra!	Simon says: look at the board!
¡Sacad los cuadernos!	Take out your exercise books!
Simon dice: ¡sacad los cuadernos!	Simon says: take out your exercise books!
Simon dice: ¡escribid en los cuadernos!	Simon says: write in your exercise books!
¡Hablad en español!	Speak in Spanish!
Simon dice: ¡hablad en español!	Simon says: speak in Spanish!
¡Levantaos!	Get up!
Simon dice: ¡levantaos!	Simon says: get up!

¿Cómo se dice en español?
Pupil's Book: Page 21.

Those using the CD Rom may click on the red controller to hear the examples pronounced.

Exercise 1.39
Pupil's Book: Page 21.

Pupils should practise their vocabulary and the phrases learnt to date by identifying a series of objects and asking the three questions for each one: *¿Cómo se dice en español? ¿Cómo se escribe? ¿Cómo se pronuncia?*

Those using the CD Rom may view a range of objects on the screen.

Exercise 1.40
Pupil's Book: Page 21; CD 1, track : 28

In this exercise, pupils hear four characters spelling out objects.

CD 1, track

1.	*José:*	*"Aquí está un alumno – a l u m n o."*
2.	*María:*	*"Aquí está una calculadora – c a l c u l a d o r a."*
3.	*David:*	*"Aquí está una pizarra – p i z a r r a."*
4.	*Ana:*	*"Aquí está un sacapuntas – s a c a p u n t a s."*

Those using the CD Rom may click on the red **?** icons to see the answers.

Exercise 1.41
Pupil's Book: Page 22; CD 1, track : 29

In this exercise, pupils read or listen to the passage and then answer the questions that follow.

CD 1, track 29:

Hoy es martes, quince de noviembre. Hay treinta alumnos en la clase. Hay dieciocho chicos y doce chicas. El profesor se llama Roberto Pérez. Tiene treinta años. Su cumpleaños es el primero de noviembre – el día de Todos los Santos. Una alumna se llama Carolina – tiene quince años. Tiene una mochila. Hay cinco libros en su mochila. Un alumno se llama José pero no tiene nada en su mochila.

Today is Tuesday, 15th November. There are 30 pupils in the class. There are 18 boys and 12 girls. The teacher is called Roberto Pérez. He is 30 years old. His birthday is 1st November – the day of *Todos los Santos*. One pupil is called Carolina. She is 15 years old. She has a schoolbag. There are 5 books in her schoolbag. One pupil is called José but he has nothing in his schoolbag.

Answers:

1.	*martes*	5.	*30*
2.	*30*	6.	*1 noviembre*
3.	*18*	7.	*5 libros*
4.	*Roberto Pérez*	8.	*José*

Those using the CD Rom may click on the red **?** icons to see the answers.

Exercise 1.42
Pupil's Book: Page 22; CD 1, track s: 30-31.

To round off this first unit, pupils prepare to conduct interviews on one another, using both the familiar and the polite forms. This is an ideal opportunity to make use of a video camera if available, allowing pupils to produce their own interviews to show to the rest of the class. The two interviews in the pupil's book may be discussed and listened to. Those using the CD Rom may watch these as simple animations on the screen.

CD 1, track 30:

Juan:	*¿Cómo te llamas?*	*What is your name?*
Ángel:	*Me llamo Ángel Hernández.*	My name is Ángel Hernández.
Juan:	*¿Cuántos años tienes?*	How old are you?
Ángel:	*Tengo dieciséis años.*	I am 16 years old.
Juan:	*¿Cuándo es tu cumpleaños?*	When is your birthday?
Ángel:	*Es el quince de marzo.*	It's the 15th March.
Juan:	*Cómo se escribe tu nombre?*	How do you spell your name?
Ángel:	*A con acento -N-G-E-L*	Á-n-g-e-l.
Juan:	*¿Y Hernández?*	And Hernández?
Ángel:	*H-E-R-N-A con acento – N-D-E-Z*	H-e-r-n-á-n-d-e-z.

CD 1, track 31:

Elena:	*¿Cómo se llama usted?*	What is your name?
Profesor:	*Me llamo Esteban Martínez.*	My name is Esteban Martínez.
Elena:	*¿Cómo se escribe Martínez?*	How do you spell Martínez?
Profesor:	*M-A-R-T-I con acento– N-E-Z*	*M-a-r-t- í with an accent -n-e-z*
Elena:	*¿Cuántos años tiene usted?*	How old are you?
Profesor:	*Tengo treinta y nueve años.*	I am 39 years old.
Elena:	*¿Cuándo es su cumpleaños?*	When is your birthday?
Profesor:	*Es el dos de mayo.*	It is the 2nd May.

Vocabulario 1.2
Pupil's Book: Page 23.

Revision of Vocabulario 1.1 might be beneficial before or after ensuring that this vocabulary has been mastered. It is hoped that the use of colour to emphasise the genders of nouns may prove beneficial.

Deberes
Pupil's Book: Page 23.

Suggestions for project work are made at the end of each unit. The use of a digital video camera would be ideal at this stage as pupils practise their language work in an interview format. Simulated interviews with famous personalities could then be conducted to practise the polite (*usted*) form.

UNIT 2

About the unit

In this unit pupils learn to talk and write about their family, friends and pets, and how to describe their appearance.

New contexts:

- other people
- descriptions of family, friends, pets
- nationalities
- Christmas, fiestas

New language content:

- regular *-AR*, *-ER* and *-IR* verbs
- possessive adjectives
- asking questions with *¿Cómo? ¿Cuánto?* and *¿Quién?*
- irregular verbs *tener* and *ser* (all persons)
- agreement of adjectives
- intensifiers (*muy, bastante*)
- numbers 1–100

Expectations

At the end of this unit most pupils will: understand and respond to descriptions of family members, including basic appearance and nationality; talk and write about families, friends and pets; count up to 100; spell some words from this unit; be more confident in their use of dictionaries to help them understand language and find new words; distinguish between *¿Quién? ¿Qué? ¿Cómo?* and *¿Cuántos/as?*; understand when and how to use different verb endings; distinguish between definite and indefinite articles.

some pupils will not have made so much progress and will: understand, with support, simple questions and answers about family members and pets; express themselves using short phrases and a limited number of adjectives.

some pupils will have progressed further and will: use a range of questions and answers in a conversation; read short passages and infer meanings from contexts; write a passage of Spanish, using a range of adjectives.

La famiia
Pupil's Book: Page 26.

Pupils are now introduced to the members of the family. Those using the CD Rom can click on the characters on the family tree and hear the following:

Mi abuelo se llama Roberto	My grandfather (top left) is called Roberto
Mi abuela se llama Laura	My grandmother (top left) is called Laura
Mi abuelo se llama Javier	My grandfather (top right) is called Javier
Mi abuela se llama Beatriz	My grandmother (top right) is called Beatriz
Mi tía se llama Carolina	My aunt (left) is called Carolina
Mi padre se llama José	My father is called José

Mi madre se llama Elena	My mother is called Elena
Mi tío se llama Juan	My uncle is called Juan
Mi tía se llama Ana	My aunt (right) is called Ana
Mi hermano se llama Raúl	My brother is called Raúl
Mi hermana se llama Susana	My sister is called Susana
Me llamo Luis	I am called Luis
Mi primo se llama Jesús	My (male) cousin is called Jesús
Mi prima se llama María	My (female) cousin is called María

Exercise 2.1
Pupil's Book: Page 26; CD 1, tracks: 32-37
CD 1, track 32:

1. **Laura:** *"¡Hola! Me llamo Laura. Tengo catorce años. En mi familia hay cinco personas: mis padres, mis dos hermanas y yo. Mi cumpleaños es el trece de mayo."*

Hi. My name is Laura. I am 14 years old. In my family there are 5 people: my parents, my two sisters and I. My birthday is on the 13th of May.

CD 1, track 33:

2. **Javier:** *"Me presento: Me llamo Javier. Tengo quince años y mi cumpleaños es el veinticuatro de junio. Somos seis en total en mi familia: tengo un hermano y dos hermanas, y mis padres claro."*

Let me introduce myself: my name is Javier. I am 15 years old and my birthday is 24th June. We are six altogether in my family: I have one brother and two sisters, and my parents of course.

CD 1, track 34:

3. **Luis** *"¡Hola! Soy Luis. Tengo dieciséis años. Mi cumpleaños es el treinta de noviembre. No tengo hermanos – soy hijo único. Hay tres personas en mi familia: mis padres y yo. Pero tengo un perro que se llama Óscar."*

Hi! I am Luis. I am 16 years old. My birthday is 30th November. I don't have any brothers – I am an only child, so there are three people in my family: my parents and I. But I have a dog called Oscar.

CD 1, track 35:

4. **Beatriz** *"Me presento – me llamo Beatriz, pero mi familia y mis amigos me llaman Bea. Tengo trece años y mi cumpleaños es el uno de marzo. Somos cuatro en mi familia: mis padres, mi hermana mayor (Luisa) y yo."*

Let me introduce myself: my name is Beatriz, but my family and my friends call me Bea. I am 13 years old and my birthday is 1st March. We are four in my family: my parents, my elder sister (Luisa) and I.

CD 1, track 36:

5. **Jesús** *"¡Hola! Me llamo Jesús. Tengo catorce años y mi cumpleaños es el diez de septiembre. Tengo una familia muy grande : somos cinco hermanos en total, tres chicos y dos chicas, y mis padres, desde luego."*

Hi! My name is Jesús. I am 14 years old and my birthday is 10th September. I have a very large family: there are five of us siblings altogether, three boys and two girls, and my parents of course.

CD 1, track 37:

6. **Montse**   *"¡Hola! Mi nombre es Montse. Tengo doce años y mi cumpleaños es el seis de enero: ¡el día de Reyes! ¡Qué chulo! ¿verdad? Hay cinco personas en mi familia. Mis padres, mi hermano menor Joaquín, mi hermana mayor Susana, y yo."*

Hi! My name is Montse. I am 12 years old and my birthday is 6th January: the day of the Kings! How cool, don't you think? There are five people in my family. My parents, my younger brother Joaquín, my elder sister Susana, and I.

Answers

Nombre	Edad	En familia	Hermanos	Hermanas	Cumpleaños
Laura	14	5	0	2	13 May
Javier	15	6	1	2	24 June
Luis	16	3	0	0	30 November
Beatriz	13	4	0	1	1 March
Jesús	14	7	2	2	10 September
Montse	12	5	1	1	6 January

Reflexive pronouns: a brief glimpse
Pupil's Book: Page 27.

Those using the CD Rom can display the information on reflexive pronouns. Clicking on each phrase allows it to be heard. Some teachers may choose to give the plural forms at this stage, using the following:

Reflexive pronouns

	Singular	**Plural**
1st person	*Me* llamo	*Nos* llamamos
2nd person	*Te* llamas	*Os* llamáis
3rd person	*Se* llama	*Se* llaman

Ejemplos:

1st person	*Me* llamo Juan	I call **myself** Juan
2nd person	*¿Cómo te llamas*	What do **you** call **yourself**?
3rd person	*Se llama Isabel*	**She** calls herself Isabel
	Mi hermano se llama Jorge	My brother calls **himself** Jorge
1st person	*Nos llamamos Juan y Laura*	We call **ourselves** Juan and Laura
2nd person	*¿Cómo os llamáis?*	What do **you** call **yourselves**?
3rd person	*Se llaman Carolina y Elena*	**They** call **themselves** Carolina and Elena

Possessive adjectives
Pupil's Book: Page 27.

Those using the CD Rom can view the information about possessive adjectives from the pupil's book. Clicking on each word or phrase allows it to be heard.

Exercise 2.2
Pupil's Book: Page 27.

Those using the CD Rom can click on the Union Flag icons to reveal the answers:
1.   He is called Roberto.
2.   I am called Raúl.
3.   My sister is called Elena.
4.   You are called Ana.
5.   My friend is called José.
6.   You are called Antonio.

Exercise: 2.3
Pupil's Book: Page 27.

Those using the CD Rom can watch a simple animation as follows before embarking on this speaking exercise:

Profesora: *"¿Cómo se llama tu hermano?"*
                    What is your brother called?

José: *"Mi hermano se llama José."*
                    My brother is called José?

Profesora: *"¿Cómo se llama tu madre?"*
                    What is your mother called?

José: *"Mi madre se llama Susana."*
                    My mother is called Susana.

Profesora: *"¿Cómo se llama tu hermana?"*
                    What is your sister called?

José: *"Mi hermana se llama Beatriz."*
                    My sister is called Beatriz.

Profesora: *"¿Cómo se llama tu abuelo?"*
                    What is your grandfather called?

José: *"Mi abuelo se llama Luis."*
                    My grandfather is called Luis.

Profesora: *"¿Cómo se llama tu tía?"*
                    What is your aunt called?

José: *"Mi tía se llama Cristina Martínez."*
                    My aunt is called Cristina Martínez.

Profesora: *"¿Cómo se escribe Martínez?"*
                    How do you write Martínez?

José: *"Se escribe M A R T I con acento N E Z."*
                    You write it Martínez.

Profesora: *"¿Cómo se llama tu primo?"*
                    What is your (male) cousin called?

José: *"No tengo primos. Pero mi prima se llama Carolina."*
                    I don't have any male cousins. But my female cousin is called Carolina.

Exercise 2.4
Pupil's Book: Page 28.

For this exercise pupils have to read the passage and work out how the named characters fit onto the family tree. The answer is shown below. Those using the CD Rom can drag the names onto the blank family tree.

Translation

Elena is the wife of Carlos and the sister of Pedro.
Carlos is the father of David.
Juan is the brother of David.
José is the grandson of Carlos.
Montse is the grand-daughter of Carlos. David is the uncle of Montse.
Montse is the wife of Jesús.

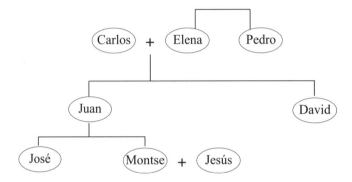

Exercise 2.5
Pupil's Book: Page 28.

Suggested answers to this are shown below. Those using the CD Rom can click on a character on the family tree to hear these phrases.

Carlos es el marido de Maribel. Es el padre de David y el abuelo de Antonio.
Carlos is the husband of Maribel. He is the father of David and the grandfather of Antonio.

Maribel es la mujer de Carlos. Es la madre de David y la abuela de Antonio.
Maribel is the wife of Carlos. She is the mother of David and the grandmother of Antonio.

Juan es el marido de María. Es el padre de Montse y el abuelo de Antonio.
Juan is the husband of Maria. He is the father of Montse and the grandfather of Antonio.

María es la mujer de Juan. Es la madre de Montse y la abuela de Antonio.
Maria is the wife of Juan. She is the mother of Montse and the grandmother of Antonio.

José es el marido de Raquel. Es el padre de Cristina y el abuelo de Juana.
José is the husband of Raquel. He is the father of Cristina and the grandfather of Juana.

Raquel es la mujer de José. Es la madre de Cristina y la abuela de Juana.
Raquel is the wife of José. She is the mother of Cristina and the grandmother of Juana.

Miguel es el marido de Carolina. Es el padre de Javier y el abuelo de Juana.
Miguel is the husband of Carolina. He is the father of Javier and the grandfather of Juana.

Carolina es la mujer de Miguel. Es la madre de Javier y la abuela de Juana.
Carolina is the wife of Miguel. She is the mother of Javier and the grandmother of Juana.

David es el hijo de Carlos y Maribel. Es el marido de Montse y el padre de Antonio. Tiene un nieto y dos nietas.
David is the son of Carlos and Maribel. He is the husband of Montse and the father of Antonio. He has one grandson and two granddaughters.

Montse es la hija de Juan y María. Es la mujer de David y la madre de Antonio. Tiene un nieto y dos nietas.
Montse is the daughter of Juan and Maria. She is the wife of David and the mother of Antonio. She has one grandson and two granddaughters.

Cristina es la hija de José y Raquel. Es la mujer de Javier y la madre de Juana. Tiene un nieto y dos nietas.
Cristina is the daughter of Jose and Raquel. She is the wife of Javier and the mother of Juana. She has one grandson and two granddaughters.

Javier es el hijo de Miguel y Carolina. Es el marido de Cristina y el padre de Juana. Tiene un nieto y dos nietas.
Javier is the son of Miguel and Carolina. He is the husband of Cristina and the father of Juana. He has one grandson and two granddaughters.

José es el hijo de Antonio y Juana. Es el hermano mayor de Raquel y Joaquín.
Jose is the son of Antonio and Juana. He is the older brother of Raquel and Joaquin.

Raquel es la hija de Antonio y Juana. Tiene un hermano mayor y una hermana menor.
Raquel is the daughter of Antonio and Juana. She has one older brother and one younger sister.

Joaquín es la hija de Antonio y Juana. Tiene un hermano mayor y una hermana mayor.
Joaquin is the daughter of Antonio and Juana. He has one older brother and one older sister.

Exercise 2.6
Pupil's Book: Page 28; CD 1, track: 38

In this exercise, pupils hear Ricardo talking about his family. Pupils then have to select *verdad* or *mentira* (true or false) for each of the six statements.

CD 1, track 38:

En mi familia hay seis personas. Mi padre que se llama Paco y mi madre que se llama Isabel. Mi abuela se llama Marisol. Tengo dos hermanas: mi hermana mayor se llama María y mi hermana menor se llama Carmen. Carmen tiene seis años y María tiene trece años. Yo me llamo Ricardo y tengo nueve años.

In my family there are six people. My father, who is called Paco, and my mother, who is called Isabel. My grandmother is called Marisol. I have two sisters: my older sister is called María and my younger sister is called Carmen. Carmen is six years old and María is thirteen years old. I am called Ricardo and I am nine years old.

	Verdad	**Mentira**
Hay 5 personas en su familia		*Mentira*
Su padre se llama Paco	*Verdad*	
Su abuela se llama María		*Mentira*
Tiene 2 hermanos		*Mentira*
Carmen tiene 13 años		*Mentira*
El chico se llama Ricardo	*Verdad*	

Those using the CD Rom can click on the **?** icons to reveal the answers.

Los verbos
Pupil's Book: Page 29.

When embarking on verbs we have deliberately given the full conjugation of the present tense. Those using the CD Rom can click on a verb form to hear it pronounced.

Exercise 2.7
Pupil's Book: Page 29.

Those using the CD Rom can display the answers by clicking on the Union Flag icons.

1.   We speak English in the school.
2.   We buy the newspapers.
3.   I work in the classroom.
4.   You study Spanish in Spain.
5.   I visit Gibraltar with my friends.
6.   They look at the male and the female teacher.
7.   You listen to your brother.
8.   You do not finish your homework.
9.   The boys do not smoke at home.
10.   The girl visits her grandfather.

Exercise 2.8
Pupil's Book: Page 30.

Those using the CD Rom can see the four verbs set out (one by one) in the present tense, with their meanings. Clicking on each verb displays that particular verb:

Visitar = to visit

	Singular		Plural	
1st person	visito	I visit	visitamos	we visit
2nd person	visitas	you visit	visitáis	you visit
3rd person	visita	he/she/it visits	visitan	they visit

Terminar = to finish

	Singular		Plural	
1st person	termino	I finish	terminamos	we finish
2nd person	terminas	you finish	termináis	you finish
3rd person	termina	he/she/it finishes	terminan	they finish

Escuchar = to listen

	Singular		Plural	
1st person	escucho	I listen	escuchamos	we listen
2nd person	escuchas	you listen	escucháis	you listen
3rd person	escucha	he/she/it listens	escuchan	they listen

Trabajar = to work

	Singular		Plural	
1st person	trabajo	I work	trabajamos	we work
2nd person	trabajas	you work	trabajáis	you work
3rd person	trabaja	he/she/it works	trabajan	they work

Exercise 2.9
Pupil's Book: Page 30.

Those using the CD Rom can display the answers by clicking on the Spanish flag icons.

1. *Visito España con mi amigo.*
2. *Mi hermano trabaja en la clase.*
3. *El abuelo compra un periódico.*
4. *Mi madre trabaja en Madrid.*
5. *Estudian español con el profesor.*

Personal pronouns
Pupil's Book: Page 30.

Those using the CD Rom can display the information on personal pronouns. Clicking on each word allows pupils to hear it pronounced.

Exercise 2.10
Pupil's Book: Page 30; CD 1, track: 39

This exercise combines the skills of accurate listening with revision of the lesson just learnt on pronouns. Those using the CD Rom can click on the **?** icons to display the missing pronouns (shown in bold below). The sentences can then be translated. Pupils should note how the genders can be distinguished in all but the first two singular persons.

CD 1, track 39:

1. **Yo** *escucho.*
2. **Tú** *estudias.*
3. **Él** *trabaja pero* **ella** *no trabaja.*
4. **Ella** *compra un periódico.*
5. **Nosotros** *visitamos al marido de Juana.*
6. **Nosotras** *visitamos a la mujer de Carlos.*
7. **Vosotros** *habláis con vuestra profesora.*
8. **Vosotras** *habláis con vuestro padre.*
9. **Ellos** *miran al profesor.*
10. **Ellas** *trabajan en un colegio.*

1. I listen.
2. You study.
3. He works but she does not work.
4. She buys a newspaper.
5. We (masculine) visit Juana's husband.
6. We (feminine) visit Carlos's wife.
7. You (masculine) speak with your teacher.
8. You (feminine) speak with your father.
9. They (masculine) look at the teacher.
10. They (feminine) work in a school.

Exercise 2.11
Pupil's Book: Page 31.

Those using the CD Rom can do this exercise as a drag and drop by dragging the correct form from the box at the bottom of the page onto the gaps in the sentences. Clicking on the Union Flag icons then allows the correct translation to be displayed.

Answers are shown in bold:

1.	Yo **compro** un periódico.	I buy a newspaper.
2.	La chica **habla** inglés.	The girl speaks English.
3.	Yo **estudio** en el colegio.	I study in the school.
4.	El profesor **fuma**.	The teacher smokes.
5.	El abuelo **visita** Málaga.	The grandfather visits Málaga.
6.	Los hermanos **escuchan**.	The brothers listen.

Exercise 2.12
Pupil's Book: Page 31.

This exercise encourages pupils to make use of their growing vocabulary of verbs and to manipulate these verbs correctly. Weaker pupils could be given a list of possible verb forms from which to select. Those using the CD Rom can do this exercise as a drag and drop, with various forms displayed on the screen from which pupils have to select the correct ones.

Answers to this are shown in bold:

1.	Nosotros **estudiamos** español.	We study Spanish.
2.	Los alumnos **visitan** Málaga.	The pupils visit Málaga.
3.	El hijo **estudia**.	The son studies.
4.	La mujer **trabaja** en una oficina.	The wife works in an office.
5.	El chico y la chica **estudian** en la clase.	The boy and the girl study in the class.

Exercise 2.13
Pupil's Book: Page 31.

Clicking on the flag icons reveals the answers:
1. We visit Barcelona.
2. He/she finishes the homework.
3. The boy buys a pen.
4. We study in the school.
5. We look at the board.
6. Hablo español en clase.
7. Los alumnos hablan inglés en casa.
8. El profesor no fuma.
9. Compro un periódico y unos bolígrafos.
10. Trabajamos en un colegio.

Exercise 2.14
Pupil's Book: Page 31.

Simple descriptions of these pictures might include:
Dos alumnos no compran un periódico.
El abuelo fuma en casa.
El hombre trabaja en una oficina.

Exercise 2.15
Pupil's Book: Page 32.

Simple descriptions of these pictures might include:
Aquí está la madre. Mira el padre y los chicos.
Aquí está la hermana. Empuja el cochecito de niño.
Aquí está el nieto. Escucha a su abuelo.

Suggestion: Pupils should be encouraged to use the vocabulary at the back of the book to find words such as push and pram.

Exercise 2.16
Pupil's Book: Page 32.

Those using the CD Rom can display the correct order by clicking on the **?** icons.

1. *hablar hablo hablas habla hablamos habláis hablan*
2. *comprar compro compras compra compramos compráis compran*
3. *fumar fumo fumas fuma fumamos fumáis fuman*
4. *estudiar estudio estudias estudia estudiamos estudiáis estudian*
5. *mirar miro miras mira miramos miráis miran*

Usted y Ustedes
Pupil's Book: Page 32.

This is a good time to discuss or revise the correct use of *Usted (Vd.)* and *Ustedes (Vds.)*. Those using the CD Rom can watch a simple animation to illustrate this point.

ER Verbs
Pupil's Book: Page 33.

Those using the CD Rom can display the information on *Comer*, and see more verbs from the vocabulary on this page laid out in the same way.

Exercise 2.17
Pupil's Book: Page 33.
Answers

1. *Mi marido **bebe** cerveza.*   My husband drinks beer.
2. *Nosotras **leemos** los libros.*   We read the books.
3. *El chico **come** el chocolate.*   The boy eats the chocolate.
4. *Los españoles **aprenden** inglés.*   The Spanish learn English.
5. *Mi abuela siempre **corre** a casa.* My grandmother always runs home.

Those using the CD Rom can display the correct verb form and the translations by clicking on the **?** icons.

Exercise 2.18
Pupil's Book: Page 33; CD 1, tracks: 40-43

In this exercise we hear four characters saying who they are and what they are doing.

CD 1, track 40:

Juan: *"Hola. Me llamo Juan. Leo un libro en mi casa."*
             Hello. My name is Juan. I read a book in my house.

CD 1, track 41:

Gloria: "*Hola. Me llamo Gloria y hoy aprendo inglés con mi abuelo.*"
Hello. My name is Gloria and today I learn English with my grandfather.

CD 1, track 42:

Cristóbal: "*Buenos días. Me llamo Cristóbal. Mis amigos y yo comemos paella.*"
Good morning. My name is Cristóbal. My friends and I eat paella.

CD 1, track 43:

Ricardo: "*Muy buenas. Me llamo Ricardo. Mis amigos beben cerveza en la plaza, pero yo estudio en el colegio.*"
Hi. My name is Ricardo. My friends drink beer in the square, but I study in the school.

Answers

1. C
2. E
3. B
4. A

Exercise 2.19
Pupil's Book: Page 34.

1. *Beber* = to drink
2. *Comer* = to eat
3. *Hablar* = to speak
4. *Mirar* = to look at
5. *Correr* = to run
6. *Leer* = to watch
7. *Hablar* = to speak
8. *Terminar* = to finish
9. *Leer* = to watch
10. *Mirar* = to look at

Those using the CD Rom can display the answers by clicking on the **?** icons.

Exercise 2.20
Pupils book: Page 34

Simple descriptions of these pictures might include:

El chico lee un libro.
Los alumnos hablan en el colegio.
¡El hombre siempre come y bebe mucho!

Vocabulario 2.1
Pupil's Book: Page 34.

Those using the CD Rom may display the words from the vocabulary on the screen.

IR Verbs
Pupil's Book: Page 35.

Those using the CD Rom can display the conjugation of vivir and four other IR verbs on the screen, as shown below.

Vivir = to live

	Singular			Plural	
1st person	vivo	I eat		vivimos	we eat
2nd person	vives	you eat		vivís	you eat
3rd person	vive	he/she/it eats		viven	they eat

Escribir = to write

	Singular			Plural	
1st person	escribo	I write		escribimos	we write
2nd person	escribes	you write		escribís	you write
3rd person	escribe	he/she/it writes		escriben	they write

Recibir = to receive

	Singular			Plural	
1st person	recibo	I receive		recibimos	we receive
2nd person	recibes	you receive		recibís	you receive
3rd person	recibe	he/she/it receives		reciben	they receive

Decidir = to decide

	Singular			Plural	
1st person	decido	I decide		decidimos	we decide
2nd person	decides	you decide		decidís	you decide
3rd person	decide	he/she/it decides		deciden	they decide

Cumplir = to reach the age of

	Singular			Plural	
1st person	cumplo	I reach the age of		cumplimos	we reach the age of
2nd person	cumples	you reach the age of		cumplís	you reach the age of
3rd person	cumple	he/she/it reaches the age of		cumplen	they reach the age of

Exercise 2.21
Pupil's Book: Page 35.

Those using the CD Rom can display the answers by clicking on the **?** icons. The translations can then also be displayed by clicking on the Union Flag icons.

1. Yo **escribo** una carta   = I write a letter.
2. Tú **decides** correr   = You decide to run.
3. Ella **cumple** 11 años   = She reaches the age of 11.
4. Nosotros **escribimos** una carta.   = We write a letter.
5. Vosotras **cumplís** 15 años.   = You reach the age of 15.
6. Ellos **reciben** unos regalos.   = They receive some gifts.

Exercise 2.22
Pupil's Book: Page 36.

Those using the CD Rom can display the answers by clicking on the **?** icons.

1.	*ellos deciden*	they decide
2.	*vosotros cumplís*	you reach the age of
3.	*nosotros recibimos*	we receive
4.	*ellas escriben*	they write
5.	*vosotros decidís*	you decide
6.	*ustedes escriben*	you write

Exercise 2.23
Pupil's Book: Page 36.

Those using the CD Rom can display the answers by clicking on the **?** icons.

Answers:

1. *recibir recibo recibes recibe recibimos recibís reciben*
2. *vivir vivo vives vive vivimos vivís viven*
3. *cumplir cumplo cumples cumple cumplimos cumplís cumplen*
4. *decidir decido decides decide decidimos decidís deciden*
5. *escribir escribo escribes escribe escribimos escribís escriben*

Exercise 2.24
Pupil's Book: Page 36.

A reading passage with questions to be answered. Those using the CD Rom can read the passage on the screen and display the answers by clicking on the **?** icons.

1. *El padre **se llama** Juan.*
2. *La **madre** es Carolina.*
3. *Madrid ésta a **50** kilómetros de Toledo.*
4. *Pedro es **el hermano**.*
5. *La hermana **se llama** Dolores.*

Irregular verbs: tener
Pupil's Book: Page 37.

Those using the CD Rom can display the information on *tener* on the screen. Clicking on each form allows that form to be heard aloud.

Exercise 2.25
Pupil's Book: Page 37. CD 1, track: 44

In this exercise, Carolina introduces her family. Pupils then fill the gaps in the sentences 1-5 below.

CD 1, track 44:

"Hola. Me llamo Carolina. Te presento a mi familia.
Mi hermano Juan. Juan tiene 11 años.
Mi hermana Gloria. Ella tiene 12 años.
Francisco, mi tío, tiene 31 años.
José y Cristina, mis primos, tienen 14 años.
Mis hermanastros Cristóbal y María tienen 17 y 13 años. Viven con mi padre en Madrid."

Translation

Hello. My name is Carolina. Let me introduce you to my family. My brother Juan. Juan is 11 years old. My sister Gloria. She is 12 years old. Francisco, my uncle, is 31 years old. José and Cristina, my cousins, are 14 years old. My step-brother and sister, Cristóbal and María are 17 and 13 years old. They live with my father in Madrid.

Answers

1. *Juan tiene **11** años. Juan es el **hermano** de Carolina.*
2. *Gloria tiene **12** años. Gloria es la **hermana** de Carolina.*
3. ***Francisco tiene** 31años. **Francisco** es el **tío** de Carolina.*
4. *José y **Cristina** tienen **14** años. Son los **primos** de Carolina.*
5. *Los hermanastros **Cristóbal** y **María** tienen **17** y **13** años. Viven con el **padre** en **Madrid**.*

Exercise 2.26
Pupil's Book: Page 37.

Those using the CD Rom can display the answers by clicking on the Union Flag icons.

1. Juan has a pen.
2. We have a magnificent teacher.
3. María and Ricardo have a house in Badajoz.
4. You have a house in Cáceres.
5. When do you have the Spanish lesson?

Ser
Pupil's Book: Page 38.

Teachers may choose to make the link between *ser* and the French être.

Ser = to be

	Spanish	French		Spanish	French
1st person	soy	je *suis*		somos	nous *sommes*
2nd person	eres	tu *es*		sois	vous *êtes*
3rd person	es	il *est*		son	ils *sont*

Exercise 2.27
Pupil's Book: Page 38.

Those using the CD Rom can display the answers by clicking on the Union Flag icons.

1. I am a pupil.
2. Juan is a teacher.
3. We are students.
4. You are my friend.
5. They are my grandparents.
6. She is my mother.

Ex 2.28
Pupil's Book: Page 38.

Those using the CD Rom can display the answers by clicking on the Spanish Flag icons.

1. *Juan es estudiante.*
2. *María y Francisco son mis abuelos.*
3. *Son mis amigos.*
4. *Ella es una alumna.*
5. *Sois mis estudiantes.*
6. *Soy vuestro profesor.*

¿Cómo eres?
Pupil's Book: Page 40.

Those using the CD Rom can display the four pictures and click the red controller buttons to hear the personal descriptions.

"Tengo el pelo negro y corto y los ojos castaños. Soy moreno."
I have black, short hair and brown eyes. I am dark.

"Tengo la cara redonda y las orejas pequeñas. Soy rubia."
I have a round face and small ears. I am blonde.

"Tengo el pelo largo y rizado, y los ojos azules. Soy pelirroja."
I have long, curly hair, and blue eyes. I am a redhead.

"Tengo la piel negra y la nariz pequeña. Tengo las cejas pobladas. Soy negro."
I have black skin and a small nose. I have bushy eye-brows. I am black.

Exercise 2.29
Pupil's Book: Page 40; CD 1, track: 45

In this exercise, Luis describes himself and his family.

CD 1, track 45:

"Hola. Me llamo Luis y vivo en Tenerife. Soy muy guapo y tengo 13 años. Hay cuatro personas en mi familia; mi padre, que se llama Javier, mi madre, que se llama Pilar, mi hermana, que se llama Ana María, y yo. Mi padre tiene 36 años. Es bastante alto, muy deportista y muy trabajador. Tiene el pelo moreno y bastante corto. Es español. Mi madre es bastante delgada y tiene 39 años. Tiene el pelo largo y tiene los ojos verdes. Mi madre es mejicana. Mi hermana tiene 7 años. ¡Es muy pesada! Tiene el pelo castaño y los ojos azules. Es bastante fea."

Hello. I am called Luis and I live in Tenerife. I am very handsome and I am 13 years old. There are four people in my family; my father, who is called Javier, my mother, who is called Pilar, my sister, who is called Ana Maria, and I. My father is 36 years old. He is quite tall, very sporty and very hardworking. His hair is brown and quite short. He is Spanish. My mother is quite thin and is 39 years old. She has long hair and she has green eyes. My mother is Mexican. My sister is 7 years old. She is very annoying! She has brown hair and blue eyes. She is quite ugly.

Answers

1. *El chico se llama **Luis**.*   The boy is called Luis.
2. *Vive en **Tenerife**.*   He lives in Tenerife.
3. *Tiene **13** años.*   He is 13 years old.

4.	*Hay 4 personas en su familia.*	There are four people in his family.
5.	*Su padre se llama Javier.*	His father is called Javier.
6.	*Su madre se llama Pilar.*	His mother is called Pilar.
7.	*Ana María es su hermana.*	Ana María is his sister.
8.	*Javier tiene 36 años.*	Javier is 36 years old.
9.	*Su madre tiene 39 años.*	His mother is 39 years old.
10.	*Su madre tiene los ojos verdes.*	His mother has green eyes.
11.	*Su hermana tiene 7 años.*	His sister is 7 years old.
12.	*Su hermana tiene el pelo castaño.*	His sister has brown hair.

Those using the CD Rom may display the answers by clicking on the **?** icons. The sentences may then be translated.

Exercise 2.30
Pupil's Book: Page 41.

Those using the CD Rom may display the answers by clicking on the **?** icons. The sentences may then be translated.

1.	*Un profesor bajo*	A short (male) teacher
2.	*Una profesora antipática*	A horrible (female) teacher
3.	*Unos hermanos pesados*	Some annoying brothers
4.	*Unas hermanas pesadas*	Some annoying sisters
5.	*La abuela delgada*	The thin grandmother
6.	*Un chico cariñoso*	An affectionate boy
7.	*Una chica guapa*	A pretty girl
8.	*Un instituto grande*	A big secondary school
9.	*Los estudiantes trabajadores*	The hard-working students
10.	*Unos abuelos simpáticos*	Some kind grandfathers

Exercise 2.31
Pupil's Book: Page 41.

In this exercise pupils practise in pairs describing themselves to their partners. Use may be made of the four descriptions at the top of page 40.

Exercise 2.32
Pupil's Book: Page 41.

Translation:

My friends are Spanish and live in Guadalupe. Juan is very fat but Gloria is thin. My Spanish teacher is very affectionate while my English teacher is very annoying.

Answers

1. The nationality of my friends is **Spanish**.
2. The fat person is called **Juan**.
3. The thin person is called **Gloria**.
4. My Spanish teacher is **very affectionate**.
5. My English teacher, however, is **very annoying**.

Suggestion: Some teachers may choose to comment on the use of *estar* in this short passage, and direct pupils ahead to page 90 of the pupil's book. Others may prefer simply to treat *está* as a piece of vocabulary to be learnt or noted down until the verb is introduced properly.

Exercise 2.33
Pupil's Book: Page 43.

Those using the CD Rom can click on the button to display a number of pets one by one. Pupils should try to name them as quickly as possible. Pupils could also bring in photos of their own pets, or cut out pictures from magazines.

Exercise 2.34
Pupil's Book: Page 43; CD 1, track: 46

In this exercise, pupils read and/or listen to the dialogue and then answer the questions that follow. Those using the CD Rom may reveal the answers to the questions by clicking on the **?** icons.

CD 1, track 46:

Roberto:	*"¿Tienes animales en casa?"*
Rafael:	*"Sí, tengo un gato, dos perros y una tortuga."*
Roberto:	*"¿Cómo se llama tu tortuga?"*
Rafael:	*"Se llama Matilde y es muy cariñosa."*
Roberto:	*"¿Y tus perros – cómo son?"*
Rafael:	*"Uno es grande y blanco; se llama Gigante. El otro es pequeño, muy delgado y marrón. Se llama Lucho. Y tú – ¿no tienes animales?"*
Roberto:	*"¡Sí claro! Tengo una mantis religiosa!"*
Rafael:	*"¡Qué miedo!"*

Translation:

Roberto:	Do you have animals at home?
Rafael:	Yes, I have a cat, two dogs and a tortoise.
Roberto:	What is your tortoise called?
Rafael:	It is called Matilde and is very affectionate.
Roberto:	And your dogs – what are they like?
Rafael:	One is big and white; he is called Gigante. The other is small, very thin and brown. He is called Lucho. And you – don't you have any animals?
Roberto:	Of course! I have a praying mantis!
Rafael:	How scary!

Answers

1.	*¿Cuántos animales tiene Rafael?*	Four
2.	*¿Quién tiene una tortuga?*	Rafael
3.	*¿Cómo es la tortuga?*	Very affectionate
4.	*¿De qué color son los perros de Rafael?*	White and brown
5.	*¿Cómo se llaman los perros?*	Gigante and Lucho
6.	*¿Qué animal tiene Roberto?*	A praying mantis

Exercise 2.35
Pupil's Book: Page 43.

Pupils talk in pairs about their pets. Pupils could also bring in photos of their own pets, or cut out pictures from magazines.

Exercise 2.36
Pupil's Book: Page 44; CD 1, tracks: 47-50.

In this exercise pupils hear four characters talk about their pets. They then fill the gaps in the questions that follow.

CD 1, track 47:

David: *"Me llamo David. En casa tengo dos peces y un perro. El perro se llama Rikki y tiene ocho años."*
I am called David. At home I have two fish and a dog. The dog is called Rikki and is eight years old.

CD 1, track 48:

Dolores: *"Hola me llamo Dolores. Vivo en Andalucía y tengo un caballo. Es negro y tiene 12 años."*
Hello. My name is Dolores. I live in Andalucia and I have a horse. It is black and is 12 years old.

CD 1, track 49:

Antonio: *"Me llamo Antonio y tengo un gato muy bonito. Es marrón y blanco y se llama Héctor."*
My name is Antonio and I have a very pretty cat. It is brown and white and is called Héctor.

CD 1, track 50:

María: *"Soy María. En mi casa tenemos dos pájaros, un hámster y una tortuga. La tortuga se llama Rapidez."*
I am María. At home we have two birds, a hamster and a tortoise. The tortoise is called Rapidez (Speed).

Answers

1. *En casa David tiene dos **peces** y **un** perro.*
    At home David has two fish and one dog.
2. *El perro se llama **Rikki**.*
    The dog is called Rikki.
3. *El perro tiene **ocho** años.*
    The dog is eight years old.
4. *Dolores vive en **Andalucia**.*
    Dolores lives in Andalucia.
5. *Dolores tiene un **caballo**.*
    Dolores has a horse.
6. *Es **negro** y tiene **12** años.*
    It is black and is 12 years old.
7. *Héctor es el **gato** de **Antonio**.*
    Hector is Antonio's cat.
8. *Héctor es **marrón** y blanco.*
    Hector is brown and white.
9. *En la casa de María hay **dos pájaros, un hámster y una tortuga**.*
    In María's house there are two birds, a hamster and a tortoise.
10. *Rapidez es una **tortuga**.*
    Rapidez is a tortoise.

Exercise 2.37
Pupil's Book: Page 44.

Those using the CD Rom may display the answers by clicking on the Spanish flag icons.

1. *Aquí está mi padre. Éste es su perro.*
2. *Mi gato se llama Senta.*
3. *Aquí están mis primos. Sus perros se llaman Pastor y Alemán.*
4. *Hola David. ¿Dónde está tu tortuga?*
5. *Aquí están Dolores y Antonio. ¿Cuántas mascotas tienen?*

Exercise 2.38
Pupil's Book: Page 44.

Those using the CD Rom may display the answers by clicking on the **?** icons and then display the translations by clicking on the Spanish flag icons.

1. *"Yo **soy** profesor"*   *I am a teacher.*
2. *"¡Usted **es** un profesor magnífico!"*   You are a magnificent teacher.
3. *"Mi amigo **es** el hijo del profesor."*   My friend is the son of the teacher.
4. *"Nosotros **somos** los campeones."*   We are the champions.
5. *"Vosotros **sois** los vencidos."*   You are the losers.

Exercise 2.39
Pupil's Book: Page 45.

Those using the CD Rom may display the answers by clicking on the Spanish flag icons.

1. *Ella tiene un caballo negro.*
2. *Somos amigos de Juan y de Christine.*
3. *Soy profesor.*
4. *Éste es el perro de mi hermano.*
5. *Son los padres de José.*

Exercise 2.40
Pupil's Book: Page 45.

Those using the CD Rom may display the answers by clicking on the Spanish flag icons.

1. *Mi hermana tiene diez años.*
2. *Soy de Barcelona.*
3. *Tenemos dos conejos y un hámster.*
4. *Mi tío es de Madrid.*
5. *Tenemos una abuela maravillosa.*

Exercise 2.41
Pupil's Book: Page 45.

Those using the CD Rom may display the answers by clicking on the Union Flag icons.

1. My father is called Juan. He is quite tall and very hard-working.
2. My friend is very lazy but very nice.
3. The Spanish teacher is quite tall, very nice and very handsome.
4. The French teacher is short, is very fat and from time to time is horrible.

Exercise 2.42
Pupil's Book: Page 45.

In this exercise pupils have to rewrite the sentences from the previous exercise but with the nouns made feminine. Father becomes mother etc. Care needs to be taken with the adjectives. Those using the CD Rom may display the answers by clicking on the **?** icons.

1. *Mi madre se llama Juana. Es bastante alta y muy trabajadora.*
2. *Mi amiga es muy perezosa pero muy simpática.*
3. *La profesora de español es bastante alta, muy simpática y muy guapa.*
4. *La profesora de francés es baja, está muy gorda y de vez en cuando es antipática.*

Suggestion: Teachers may choose to highlight the forms that will change, or ask pupils to do this for themselves before they start.

Exercise 2.43
Pupil's Book: Page 45.

Those using the CD Rom may display the answers by clicking on the Union Flag icons.

1. You have a Spanish husband.
2. I am big and hard-working.
3. You are short and fat.
4. My friend is French and lazy.
5. My brother is nice and affectionate.

Exercise 2.44
Pupil's Book: Page 45.

Another exercise in manipulation of forms, this time making them plural. Those using the CD Rom may display the answers by clicking on the **?** icons.

1. *Vosotras tenéis unos maridos españoles.*
2. *Somos grandes y trabajadores.*
3. *Sois bajos y gordos.*
4. *Mis amigos son franceses y vagos.*
5. *Mis hermanos son simpaticos y cariñosos.*

Suggestion: Teachers may choose to highlight the forms that will change, or ask pupils to do this for themselves before they start.

Exercise 2.45
Pupil's Book: Page 46; CD 1, track: 51

Pupils listen to the audio track and fill in the gaps in the table. Those using the CD Rom may do this as a drag and drop exercise.

CD 1, track 51:

La hierba es verde.	The grass is green.
El cielo es azul.	The sky is blue.
El sol es amarillo.	The sun is yellow.
El hámster es marrón.	The hamster is brown.
El caballo es negro.	The horse is black.
La nieve es blanca.	The snow is white.

Answers

La hierba	verde
El cielo	azul
El sol	amarillo
El hámster	marrón
El caballo	negro
La nieve	blanca

La corrida de toros
Pupil's Book: Page 46-7.

The subject of bull-fighting is an emotive one and teachers will choose how best to approach it. A discussion of the sport gives ample opportunity for highlighting differences between cultures, prejudice, animal rights, exorbitant sums earned by sports personalities, etc.

Exercise 2.46
Pupil's Book: Page 47.

In this exercise pupils look at the pictures of the bull-fighter El Juli and answer the questions. Those using the CD Rom may display the answers by clicking on the **?** icons.

1.   *El toro es negro.*
2.   *La chaqueta de El Juli es dorada.*
3.   *La corbata es roja.*
4.   *La muleta es rosa y amarilla.*

Exercise 2.47
Pupil's Book: Page 47.

In this exercise, pupils should talk in pairs about their favourite colours.

Exercise 2.48
Pupil's Book: Page 48.

In this exercise, pupils read about the bullfighter El Juli and then answer in English the questions that follow. Those using the CD Rom can display the answers by clicking on the **?** icons.

Answers

1.   One of the most famous bullfighters in Spain.
2.   El Juli.
3.   They are El Juli's two brothers.
4.   These days El Juli fights in the bullring in Mexico and he is very famous in Mexico.
5.   Mexico has the biggest bullring in the world.
6.   A gold jacket and white socks.
7.   His fans.
8.   He goes to a hotel and has supper with his friends.

Exercise 2.49
Pupil's Book: Page 48.

This screen displays the six pictures from the pupil's book. Pupils should complete the phrases. Examples are given below:

1. *Mi hermano tiene un caballo grande.*
   My brother has a big horse.

2. *Mi abuela tiene un gato simpático.*
   My grandmother has a nice cat.

3. *Mi tía tiene un perro bonito.*
   My aunt has a nice-looking dog.

4. *Mi madre tiene un perro muy antipático.*
   My mother has a very horrible dog.

5. *Mi hermana tiene dos peces cariñosos.*
   My sister has two affectionate fish.

6. *Mi amigo tiene un padre muy vago.*
   My friend has a very lazy father.

Las nacionalidades
Pupil's Book: Page 50.

The fact that nationalities are adjectives will need to be stressed, along with the fact that they do not use capital letters as in English.

Exercise 2.50
Pupil's Book: Page 50.

Those using the CD Rom can display the answers by clicking on the Union Flag icons.

1. Juan is Spanish.
2. The teachers are Portugese.
3. My Irish friend is lazy.
4. My Spanish friend is affectionate.
5. My English teachers are hard-working.
6. David is Welsh.
7. My English teacher is fat.
8. My Spanish teacher is handsome.
9. My brother is annoying.
10. Many Spaniards are affectionate.

Exercise 2.51
Pupil's Book: Page 51.

Those using the CD Rom can display the answers by clicking on the Spanish flag icons.

1. *¿Es usted español?*
2. *Éste es José. Él es portugués.*
3. *Mis padres son franceses.*
4. *Mi profesor es americano.*
5. *Cinco alumnos en mi clase son ingleses, tres son irlandeses y dos son galeses.*
6. *Siete alumnos son escoceses, nueve son indios y dos son chinos.*
7. *Mi madre es francesa y mi padre es italiano.*
8. *Aquí están mis amigos, Juan y Cristina. Son españoles.*

Exercise 2.52
Pupil's Book: Page 51; CD 1, tracks: 52-55

This screen allows pupils to hear the four characters talking about their families. They should write notes about each one and the results can be discussed as a group, or pupils may be asked to write down what they have learnt in Spanish or English. Those using the CD Rom may display the translations for each character by clicking on the **?** icons.

CD 1, track 52:

Ignacio:
"Hola. Me llamo Ignacio y soy de Madrid. Soy alto y deportista pero según mis amigos soy vago de vez en cuando."
Hello. I am called Ignacio and I am from Madrid. I am tall and sporty but according to my friends I am sometimes lazy.

CD 1, track 53:

Teresa:
"Hola. Soy Teresa y vivo en Sevilla. Hay cinco personas en mi familia. Mi padre, mi madre, mi hermano, y mi hermana. Mi hermano mayor se llama Jorge y ésta muy gordo. Mi hermana menor se llama Nuria y ¡es muy pesada!"
Hello. I am Teresa and I live in Seville. There are five people in my family. My father, my mother, my brother and my sister. My older brother is called Jorge and is very fat. My smaller sister is called Nuria and is very annoying!

CD 1, track 54:

Eduardo:
"Yo soy Eduardo y tengo veinticuatro años. Vivo en una casa muy grande en el centro de Madrid. Soy rubio con los ojos castaños. Mi padre es español pero mi madre es argentina. Mi madre es guapa y simpática. Mi novia se llama María. Es morena."
I am Eduardo and I am 24 years old. I live in a very big house in the centre of Madrid. I am fair with brown eyes. My father is Spanish but my mother is Argentinian. My mother is pretty and nice. My girlfriend is called Maria. She is dark.

CD 1, track 55:

Elizabeth:
"¡Buenos días! Me llamo Elizabeth y soy inglesa pero vivo en España. Somos tres en la familia – mis padres y yo. Vivimos en un apartamento grande en Toledo. Mis padres son muy simpáticos. Mi madre es alta y delgada. Mi padre es bajo."
Good morning! I am called Elizabeth and I am English but I live in Spain. There are three of us in the family – my parents and I. We live in a big apartment in Toledo. My parents are very nice. My mother is tall and slim. My father is short.

Exercise 2.53
Pupil's Book: Page 51.

In this exercise pupils ask and answer a number of questions about themselves, their family and friends.

Exercise 2.54
Pupil's Book: Page 52; CD 1, track: 56

In this exercise six characters introduce themselves and say which languages they speak. Those using the CD Rom may click on the **?** icon to reveal the answers.

CD 1, track 56:

1. **Carlos:** *"Soy argentino pero vivo en Miami, en los Estados Unidos. Hablo dos idiomas: el español y el inglés."*

2. **Juanita:** *"Yo soy española. Vivo en Barcelona. Hablo catalán y castellano también."*

3. **Patricia:** *"Hola. Me llamo Patricia y soy irlandesa pero vivo en Madrid con mis padres. Hablo inglés, claro, y ahora aprendo español."*

4. **David:** *"Hola. Yo soy David. Soy inglés y estudio en la Universidad en Granada. Hablo tres idiomas: el inglés, el español y también el francés."*

5. **Monique:** *"Hola. Me llamo Monique. Soy francesa. Sólo hablo francés. Pues...aprendo español en el colegio pero lo hablo mal."*

6. **Ralph:** *Soy italiano de padres alemanes. Hablo italiano, alemán y también español.*

Answers:

1. Spanish, English
2. Catalan, Castilian
3. English, Spanish
4. English, Spanish, French
5. French, Spanish
6. Italian, German, Spanish

Exercise 2.55
Pupil's Book: Page 52.

In this exercise pupils read a short passage about three famous Spanish personalities and have to guess who they are. Licence is required for the fact that the past tense cannot yet be used.

1. He is a famous man in Spanish literature. He is very tall and very slim. He has a horse called Rocinante. He also has a very fat friend called Sancho. Who is he?

   Answer: Don Quijote.

2. He is a famous Spanish painter. He is called Pablo and he lives in Málaga in 1881. He is a short man and is very fat. He also lives in Paris. He paints a famous painting called Guernica. Who is he?

   Answer: Pablo Picasso.

3. His name is Cristóbal (Christopher). He is a famous Spanish sailor. He lives in Spain and Portugal. In 1492 he discovers Cuba and La Española. Who is he?

   Answer: Cristóbal Colon (Christopher Columbus)

Exercise 2.56
Pupil's Book: Page 53.
Answers

1. *ochenta y siete*
2. *setenta y seis*
3. *sesenta y cinco*
4. *noventa y dos*
5. *cuarenta y cuatro*

Exercise 2.57
Pupil's Book: Page 53.

1.   thirty-two
2.   forty-one
3.   ninety-four
4.   seventy-five
5.   fifty-six

Exercise 2.58
Pupil's Book: Page 53.

This screen displays the mathematical problems from the pupil's book. The point of the exercise is to get pupils to practise using their numbers up to 100 and it is accepted that the sums involved are a good deal harder than was perhaps necessary. Indeed without discreet use of brackets, they won't come out at all, and for this we apologise! Many thanks to Louise Martine for the following calculations:

E.g.: 21: $(3 \times 6) + 9 - 6 = 21$

1.   46: $33 + (21-(2 \times 4)) = 46$
2.   40: $(9 + 7 + 4) \times 2 = 40$
3.   43: $((16 / 4) \times 5) + 23 = 43$
4.   67: $74 - ((19-14) + 2) = 67$
5.   76: $((8-6) \times 7) + 62 = 76$

Exercise 2.59
Pupil's Book: Page 53; CD 1, tracks: 57-60

In this exercise, characters give their phone numbers to a friend. This exercise acts as valuable practice to the necessary skill of extracting limited but specific information from a longer spoken sequence, as well as providing valuable revision of numbers. Most pupils will probably be taught to listen out only for the information they are required to collect. The more able will have little difficulty in listening to and understanding the entire conversation. The Spanish tendency to group numbers in pairs makes this type of exercise harder than it perhaps might otherwise be.

CD 1, track 57:

1.   **Carolina**
      Carolina: *"¡Hola! ¿Qué tal?"*
      Miguel: *"Bien, gracias. ¿Cómo te llamas?"*
      Carolina: *"Me llamo Carolina y mi número de teléfono es 23-26-87."*

Translation:

      Carolina: Hi. How are you doing?
      Miguel: Well, thanks. What are you called?
      Carolina: I am called Carolina and my telephone number is 23-26-87.

CD 1, track 58:

2.   **Miguel**
      Francisco: *"¡Buenos días! ¿Cómo te llamas?"*
      Miguel: *"Me llamo Miguel."*
      Francisco: *"¿Cuál es tu número de teléfono?"*
      Miguel: *"Mi número de teléfono es 66-19-95."*

Translation:

Francisco:	Good morning! What are you called?
Miguel:	I am called Miguel.
Francisco:	What is your telephone number?
Miguel:	My telephone number is 66-19-95.

CD 1, track 59:

3. Francisco

Francisco:	*"¡Buenas tardes!, Elena."*
Elena:	*"¡Buenas tardes!, Francisco. ¿Cuál es tu número de teléfono?"*
Francisco:	*"Mi número de teléfono? Un momento...ah 034-89-82. Hasta luego!"*
Elena:	*"Hasta luego."*

Translation:

Francisco:	Good afternoon, Elena!
Elena:	Good afternoon, Francisco. What is your telephone number?
Francisco:	My telephone number? One moment...ah, 034-89-82. See you later!
Elena:	See you later!

CD 1, track 60:

4. Antonio

Elena:	*"¡Buenas noches, Antonio!¿Cuál es su número de teléfono?"*
Antonio:	*"Mi número de teléfono es 41-92-37. Adiós."*
Elena:	*"Adiós, Antonio."*

Translation:

Elena:	Good evening, Antonio! What is your telephone number?
Antonio:	My telephone number is 41-92-37. Goodbye.
Elena:	Goodbye, Antonio.

Answers

1.	*Carolina*	23-26-87
2.	*Miguel*	66-19-95
3.	*Francisco*	034-89-82
4.	*Antonio*	41-92-37

Exercise 2.60
Pupil's Book: Page 54.

This exercise provides practice at extracting written information from a form or table.

1. Cristóbal Fernández García
2. Salou
3. 14
4. 23rd April
5. Spain

Exercise 2.61
Pupil's Book: Page 54.

This screen displays Vanessa's's identity card and the questions below it. Clicking on the answers icon reveals the answers to the questions.

1. Fleitas Diaz
2. Moya
3. 28 diciembre
4. 24 (in 2003)
5. Luis Manuel
6. Maria Delia
7. C/ Bolivia 11- 2

Exercise 2.62
Pupil's Book: Page 55; CD 1, tracks: 61-64

In this exercise four characters give personal information about themselves and pupils have to fill in identity cards for them.

CD 1, track 61:

Charo: *"Hola. Me llamo Charo Domingo Chaves. Vivo en Madrid en la Calle Juan Duque número 4, primero A. El código postal es dos ocho cero cero cinco. Soy estudiante y tengo veinticinco años. Mi cumpleaños es el veintitrés de junio. Soy española."*
Hello. My name is Charo Domingo Chaves. I live in Madrid in Juan Duque street, number 4, 1st floor, Flat A. The postcode is 28005. I am a student and I am 25 years old. My birthday is 23rd June. I am Spanish.

CD 1, track 62:

Francisco: *"Buenas tardes. Mi nombre es Francisco Beloso Domínguez. Soy de Cádiz, en el sur de España, pero vivo en Barcelona, en la Calle Balmes, número 16, en el segundo piso. El código postal es cuatro cero cinco cero seis. Tengo catorce años y mi cumpleaños es el uno de enero. Mi padre es colombiano y mi madre es de Sevilla pero yo soy español."*
Good afternoon. My name is Franciso Beloso Domínguez. I am from Cádiz, in the south of Spain, but I live in Barcelona, in the Calle Balmes, number 16, on the second floor. The postal code is 40506. I am 14 years old and my birthday is 1st January. My father is Colombian and my mother is from Seville but I am Spanish.

CD 1, track 63:

Óscar: *"Hola. Me llamo Óscar Blanco Martínez. Soy argentino pero vivo con mis tíos en España.Mi dirección es Plaza Pío, número doce, Málaga, dos nueve cero cero siete. Estudio en la Universidad. Mi cumpleaños es el mes que viene, el quince, y cumplo diecinueve años."*
Hello. My name is Óscar Blanco Martínez. I am Argentinian but I live with my cousins in Spain. My address is No. 12 Plaza Pío, Málaga, 29007. I study at the university. My birthday is next month, the 15th, and I reach the age of 19.

CD 1, track 64:

Mónica: *"Hola. Soy Mónica Nuevo Zamora y soy de Valladolid. Vivo en la Calle las Mercedes, número once, quinto B. El código postal es 47006. Nací el tres de mayo de mil novecientos noventa. Soy española."*

Hello. I am Mónica Nuevo Zamora and I am from Valladolid. I live in the Calle las Mercedes, number 11, 5 B. The postcode is 47006. I was born 3rd May 1990. I am Spanish.

N.B. The details on this last character will depend on when this exercise is done; her age will update by reference to the system clock.

Exercise 2.63
Pupil's Book: Page 55.

In this exercise pupils have to allocate a series of Spanish words to groups. Those using the CD Rom can do this on the screen by dragging the various words into the appropriate column of the table.

meses	días	estaciones	colores	equipo	nacionalidades
enero	jueves	primavera	gris	rotulador	español
noviembre	lunes	invierno	naranja	pizarra	alemán
julio	domingo	verano	rojo	bolígrafo	argentino
diciembre				silla	inglés
				regla	

Exercise 2.64
Pupil's Book: Page 55.

1. *La madre de Francisco.*
2. *Los profesores de Elena.*
3. *La hija de mi tía.*
4. *La familia de tu amigo.*
5. *La mochila de su hermana.*
6. *El bolígrafo del chico.*
7. *La regla de la chica.*
8. *Los libros de mis padres.*
9. *Las tijeras de los alumnos.*
10. *Los deberes de su amigo/amiga.*

Exercise 2.65
Pupil's Book: Page 55.

1. *Mi padre se llama Robert.*
2. *Mi abuelo se llama Angel.*
3. *Maribel es la nieta de Gloria.*
4. *Rafael es mi hermanastro.*
5. *Su tío David es el hermano de su madre.*
6. *Jorge es el hijo de Miguel.*

La Navidad
Pupil's Book: Page 56.

The end of unit section on Christmas gives ample scope for discussion and project work on the similarities and differences between the ways that Christmas is celebrated in Spain and the UK.

UNIT 3

About this unit

In this unit pupils learn to talk about which school subjects they like, dislike and prefer, giving simple reasons. They will learn to comment orally and in writing about their school timetable and the times of different activities, including mealtimes. They will extend their learning about how to use a dictionary or glossary, and enhance memory work.

Where the unit fits in

This unit introduces simple opinions and preferences. It extends the scope for pupils to ask for and give personal information in the context of school, and develops their skills in applying prior learning, especially verbs. The unit introduces regular -*er* verbs and radical-changing verbs.

New contexts:

- school subjects and timetables
- telling the time
- mealtimes and simple items of food and drink

New language content:

- expressing likes, dislikes and preferences using *(no) gustar (mucho, nada)*
- radical- (stem) changing verbs *e* ➝ *ie*, eg *preferir (ie)* and *pensar (ie)*
- adverbs of frequency (*normalmente, siempre, algunas veces*)
- asking the question *¿A qué hora?*
- the irregular verb *hacer*

Expectations

At the end of this unit most pupils will: make statements and ask questions about which subjects they like, dislike and prefer; understand and use radical-changing verbs; identify a radical-changing verb from its dictionary entry; describe their timetable and give times in response to questions such as *¿Qué haces a las ... ?*; describe their school, and say how many teachers and pupils it has; describe and ask questions about mealtimes.

Some pupils will not have made so much progress and will: use set phrases to express likes and dislikes about school subjects; understand expressions of time and ask other people when they have certain lessons; fill in a timetable with their subjects; copy phrases, making appropriate substitutions to describe mealtimes, or write phrases generally accurately from memory.

Some pupils will have progressed further and will: express opinions by saying why they like or dislike something, using *pensar* and adjectives; write compound sentences, largely from memory, describing their school day and mealtimes; use a dictionary or glossary to find the words they need.

Las asignaturas
Pupil's Book: Page 60.

Those using the CD Rom can display the subjects on the screen. Clicking on each one allows pupils to hear the subject pronounced in Spanish.

Exercise 3.1
Pupil's Book: Page 61; CD 1, track 65

In this screen, the four characters give their favourite subjects. Clicking on the answer icon reveals the favourite subject of each one.

Track 65:

Monica: *"Yo estudio historia y ciencias pero mi asignatura preferida es el inglés."*

Fernando: *"Yo estudio matemáticas y religión pero mi asignatura preferida es la informática."*

Teresa: *"Yo estudio latín y griego pero mi asignatura preferida es la educación física."*

Ignacio: *"Yo estudio historia, religión y alemán pero mi asignatura preferida es el dibujo."*

Answers:

Mónica: I study history and sciences but my favourite subject is English.

Fernando: I study maths and religious studies but my favourite subject is I.T.

Teresa: I study Latin and Greek but my favourite subject is P.E.

Ignacio: I study history, R.S. and German but my favourite subject is art.

Exercise 3.2
Pupil's Book: Page 61.
Answers:

1. I study many subjects. English is useful, physics is boring but I am good at History because the teacher explains very well.
2. My favourite subject is Geography because it is very easy.
3. I am useless at French.
4. I think that Maths is very interesting, but I think that English is very boring.
5. I am good at History. I think that it is interesting and I get on well with the teacher.

Those using the CD Rom can display the sentences on the screen. Clicking on the Union Flag icons displays the answers.

Exercise 3.3
Pupil's Book: Page 61.

Before pupils try this speaking exercise, teachers may wish to rehearse a typical conversation for them to imitate. Those using the CD Rom can listen to an example of someone giving their favourite subject, etc. as follows.

*"Yo estudio **9** asignaturas. Mi asignatura preferida son las **matemáticas** porque son muy **útiles**. Se me da fatal **el latín** porque es **aburrido**."*

I study 9 subjects. My favourite subject is Maths because it is very useful. I am bad at

Latin because it is boring.

Exercise 3.4
Pupil's Book: Page 61.

1. José studies Geography and Sciences but his favourite subject is French.
2. Cristina studies Maths and Physics but her favourite subject is I.T.
3. Juan and Pepe study many subjects. Juan's favourite subject is English and Pepe's favourite subject is French.
4. Miguel thinks that Maths is very amusing because it is very easy.
5. Hello. My name is María. I study many subjects. I am bad at German and Latin but I think that Maths is very interesting and very useful.

Those using the CD Rom can display the correct answers by clicking on the Union Flag icons.

Gustar
Pupil's Book: Page 62.

This screen displays the information about *gustar*, with the indirect pronouns, together with the examples below:

Me gusta la historia	I like History
Te gusta el dibujo	You like drawing
Le gusta el inglés	He likes English
Nos gusta la geografía	We like Geography
Os gustan las matemáticas	You like Maths
Les gusta el español	They like Spanish

Exercise 3.5
Pupil's Book: Page 63; CD1, track 66

In this exercises, pupils listen to a series of sentences and have to fill in the missing phrases (marked in bold):

CD 1, track 66:

1. *¡Hola! Me llamo Enrique. Me **gustan** los deportes.*
2. *Buenos días. Me llamo Helena. **Me gusta** el alemán.*
3. *José ¡Hola! ¿**Qué tal?** Me gustan **los deportes y la tecnología**.*
4. *Ana estudia la química pero **no le gusta la biología**.*
5. *¡Muy buenas! Me llamo **Cristina**. Me **gustan** las ciencias pero no **me gustan las matemáticas**.*

Translations:

1. Hello. My name is Enrique. I like sport.
2. Good morning. My name is Helena. I like German.
3. José. Hello. How are you? I like sport and I.T.
4. Ana studies chemistry but she doesn't like biology.
5. Hi! My name is Cristina. I like Science but I don't like Maths.

Those using the CD Rom can display the correct answers by clicking on the Union Flag icons.

Exercise 3.6
Pupil's Book: Page 63.

In this exercise, pupils talk in pairs about those subjects they like and those they don't.
Those using the CD Rom can listen to the example as set out in the pupil's book.

Exercise 3.7
Pupil's Book: Page 63.

1. *Me gusta el colegio.*
2. *No me gustan los deberes.*
3. *Me gustan los idiomas.*
4. *No me gustan las matemáticas.*
5. *¿Qué asignatura te gusta?*
6. *Le gustan la historia y la geografía, ¿verdad?*
7. *A él le gusta el dibujo.*
8. *A ella le gustan los deportes.*
9. *¿Qué asignaturas les gustan Vds.?*
10. *No nos gustan las ciencias porque no nos gusta el profesor.*
11. *Chicos, ¿qué asignaturas os gustan?*
12. *Les gusta la informática, pero no les gusta la religión.*

Those using the CD Rom can display the correct answers by clicking on the Spanish flag icons.

Exercise 3.8
Pupil's Book: Page 63.

1. We do not eat paella.
2. We do not drink coca cola in the canteen.
3. I do not like Chemistry.
4. I do not work at home.
5. My friends smoke in the library.
6. You like the school, don't you?
7. I do not have my exercise book.
8. We do not live in Barcelona.
9. My parents are not from Ireland.
10. I am not 15 years old.

Those using the CD Rom can display the correct answers by clicking on the Union Flag icons.

Exercise 3.9
Pupil's Book: Page 64; CD 1, tracks: 67-71

In this exercise pupils listen to the audio tracks and then fill in the table of likes and dislikes.

Track 67:

Enrique: *"Me llamo Enrique. Me gusta la informática pero no me gusta el dibujo."*
                 My name is Enrique. I like I.T. but I don't like Art.

Track 68:

Helena: *"Me llamo Helena. No me gusta la historia pero me gustan los deportes."*
                 My name is Helena. I don't like History but I do like sport.

Track 69:

Ana: *"Me llamo Ana. Me gusta el inglés pero no me gusta el francés."*
                 My name is Ana. I like English but I do not like French.

Track 70:

Verónica: *"Me llamo Verónica. Me gustan las matemáticas pero no me gustan las ciencias."*
My name is Veronica. I like Maths but I do not like Science.

Track 71:

Alberto: *"Me llamo Alberto. Me gusta mucho el español pero no me gusta nada la geografía."*
My name is Alberto. I really like Spanish but I don't like Geography at all.

Nombre	J *Le gusta(n)*	L *No le gusta(n)*
Enrique	la informática	el dibujo
Helena	los deportes	la historia
Ana	el inglés	el francés
Verónica	las matemáticas	las ciencias
Alberto	el español	la geografía

Those using the CD Rom can display the answers by clicking on the **?** icons.

Exercise 3.10
Pupil's Book: Page 64.

1.   *No estudio nada de latín.*
2.   *No vivimos en España.*
3.   *Mi hermana no estudia mucho.*
4.   *No aprendo el alemán.*
5.   *No hablamos nada el francés.*
6.   *Me gusta mucho la historia.*
7.   *Mi director es muy pesado.*
8.   *A mi hermano le gustan mucho las matemáticas*
9.   *A mis amigos no les gustan nada los deportes.*
10.   *No me gustan nada las ciencias.*

¿Qué piensas?
Pupil's Book: Page 64.

Those using the CD Rom can display the information on giving opinions from the pupil's book. Clicking on the phrases allows pupils to hear the examples.

Other phrases that pupils might consider include:

Creo que el libro es interesante.	I think that the book is interesting.
Pienso que el libro es interesante.	I think that the book is interesting.
Opino que el libro es interesante.	I think that the book is interesting.
En mi opinión el director es pesado.	In my opinion the headmaster is annoying.
A mi juicio el director es pesado.	In my judgement the headmaster is annoying.

Exercise 3.11
Pupil's Book: Page 65; CD 1, tracks: 72-76

In this exercise pupils hear five characters give their opinions on a range of subjects. They should make notes about what they hear and discuss these in pairs or with the rest of the class. Those using the CD Rom can display the translations by clicking on the ? icons.

Track 72:

1. **Marisa:** *¡Hola! Soy Marisa. Yo prefiero el inglés. Pienso que las clases son muy interesantes y me llevo bien con el profesor.*

    Hello. I am Marisa. I prefer English. I think that the lessons are very interesting and I get on well with the teacher.

Track 73:

2. **Félix:** *Me llamo Félix. No me gusta nada la física porque es aburrida . Opino que mi asignatura preferida es la historia ya que el profesor explica muy bien.*

    My name is Félix. I don't like Physics at all because it is boring. I think that my favourite subject is History because the teacher explains very well.

Track 74:

3. **Manuel:** *Soy Manuel. En mi opinión las matemáticas son muy interesantes y me llevo bien con el profesor. ¡Es muy divertido!*

    I am Manuel. In my opinion Maths is very interesting and I get on well with the teacher. He is very amusing!

Track 75:

4. **Begoña:** *Me llamo Begoña. Mi asignatura preferida es el dibujo porque pienso que es fácil. No me gustan nada los deportes – ¡creo que son estúpidos!*

    My name is Begoña. My favourite subject is Art because I think that it is easy. I don't like sport at all – I think it's stupid!

Track 76:

5. **Harold:** *Me llamo Harold . Soy inglés y vivo aquí en Marbella. En mi colegio, prefiero las matemáticas ya que el profesor es muy divertido. No me llevo bien con el profesor de educación física – es muy pesado y no me gustan los deportes.*

    My name is Harold. I am English and I live here in Marbella. In my school I prefer Maths because the teacher is very amusing. I don't get on well with my Physics teacher – he is very annoying and I don't like Sport.

E.C.A*
Pupil's Book: Page 65.

This section is useful for encouraging pupils to expand on their answers and introduce opinions and reasons. Those using the CD Rom can hear the three types of answer, E, C and A* by clicking on the phrases on the screen.

E grade answer: Yes.

C grade answer: Yes, I want to learn Spanish.

A* grade answer: Yes, I want to learn Spanish because it is very interesting. I think that it is a very useful subject and I get on well with my teacher. He is brilliant!

Exercise 3.12
Pupil's Book: Page 65.

This exercise gives practice at giving reasons and opinions. Those using the CD Rom can see and listen to the three types of answer, E, C and A*, displayed in a table:

1. *¿Te gusta el colegio?*
    E grade answer: *Sí.*
    C grade answer: *Si, me gusta el colegio.*
    A* grade answer: *Sí, me gusta el colegio porque es muy interesante. Creo que las asignaturas son muy útiles y me llevo bien con mis profesores – ¡son estupendos!*

2. *¿Son simpáticos tus profesores?*
    E grade answer: *Sí.*
    C grade answer: *Si, son simpáticos mis profesores.*
    A* grade answer: *Sí, son simpáticos mis profesores – ¡son estupendos! Me llevo bien con mi profesor de historia; en mi opinión explica muy bien.*

3. *¿Te gusta la Navidad?*
    E grade answer: *Sí.*
    C grade answer: *Si, me gusta la Navidad.*
    A* grade answer: *Sí, me gusta la Navidad porque toda la familia está en el país y recibimos muchos regalos! ¡Me gusta mucho la comida, especialmente la torta*!*

Pupils may need to be given the meaning of *la torta* (= cake).

Exercise 3.13
Pupil's Book: Page 65.

More practice, as above.

Radical changing verbs: e → ie
Pupil's Book: Page 66.

This is a good time to revise the three regular verb conjugations learnt so far, before embarking on radical changing verbs. Those using the CD Rom can click on each verb form to hear it pronounced and pupils should be encouraged to learn the pattern (i.e. that all persons singular and the 3rd person plural are the ones where the radical change occurs).

Exercise 3.14
Pupil's Book: Page 66.

1. **Fregar (ie)**
    friego   *fregamos*
    friegas   *fregáis*
    friega   *friegan*

2. **Perder (ie)**
    pierdo   *perdemos*
    pierdes   *perdéis*
    pierde   *pierden*

3. **Mentir (ie)**
    miento   *mentimos*
    mientes   *mentís*
    miente   *mienten*

Exercise 3.15
Pupil's Book: Page 66.

This exercise can be done as a speaking exercise or a written one. Where a question is posed, pupils may wish to answer the question from their own point of view. Those using the CD Rom can display the translations by clicking on the Spanish flag icons.

1. *¿Prefieres español o alemán?*
2. *Ella piensa que la historia es interesante.*
3. *Prefieren Ciencias porque piensan que es fácil.*
4. *¿Por qué quieres trabajar en casa?*
5. *Pensamos que los profesores en nuestra escuela prefieren enseñar a los alumnos mayores.*

La hora
Pupil's Book: Page 67; CD 1, track: 77

This track allows pupils to hear the twelve hours of the day said aloud. screen allows pupils to adjust a clock and hear the corresponding time spoken out loud. Clicking on the clock face on any of the hours (1-12) changes the time to that hour (o'clock only):

Track 77:

A la una   *A las siete*
A las dos   *A las ocho*
A las tres   *A las nueve*
A las cuatro   *A las diez*
A las cinco   *A las once*
A las seis   *A las doce*

¿Qué hora es?
Pupil's Book: Page 67.

Once pupils can cope with the hours, they can learn to add the quarter hours to their telling of the time. Those using the CD Rom can use the interactive clock face which can be altered to any time of day for practice.

Exercise 3.16
Pupil's Book: Page 67.

This exercise encourages pupils to practise saying and writing the time. Those using the CD Rom can hear the times of day correctly pronounced.

1. *Es la una y cuarto.*
2. *Son las seis menos cuarto.*
3. *Son las tres y media.*
4. *Son las dos y cuarto.*
5. *Son las siete.*
6. *Son las diez menos cuarto.*
7. *Son las nueve.*
8. *Son las ocho y media.*
9. *Son las cinco menos cuarto.*
10. *Son las once y media.*

Exercise 3.17
Pupil's Book: Page 68.
Answers:

1.	1.45		6.	11.30
2.	1.30		7.	11.45
3.	6.00		8.	3.00
4.	5.15		9.	2.30
5.	4.15		10.	4.00

Those using the CD Rom can display the answers by clicking on the **?** icons.

Exercise 3.18
Pupil's Book: Page 68.

This exercise allows pupils to practise asking and answering questions about the school timetable. Those using the CD Rom can hear examples of answers to the questions as follows:

1. *¿A qué hora llegas al colegio?*
   When do you arrive at the school?
   Llego al colegio a las ocho y cuarto.
   I arrive at the school at 8.15.

2. *¿Cuántas clases de historia tienes?*
   How many History lessons do you have?
   Tengo tres clases de historia cada semana.
   I have three History lessons each week.

3. *¿Cuántas clases de inglés tienes?*
   How many English lessons do you have?
   Tengo cuatro clases de inglés cada semana.
   I have four English lessons each week.

4. *¿Cuántas clases de geografía tienes?*
   How many Geography lessons do you have?
   Tengo dos clases de geografía cada semana.
   I have 2 Geography lessons each week.

5. *¿Cuándo tienes historia?*
   When do you have History?
   Tengo historia los lunes, los martes y los jueves.
   I have History on Mondays, Tuesdays and Thursdays.

6. *¿A qué hora tienes inglés?*
   At what time do you have English?
   Los lunes y los martes tengo inglés a las nueve; y los jueves y los viernes lo tengo a las once y media .
   On Mondays and Tuesdays I have English at 9.00; and on Thursdays and Fridays I have it at 11.30.

7. *¿Dónde y cuándo tienes geografía?*
   Where and when do you have Geography?
   Tengo geografía los lunes y los martes en el aula del Sr. Beloso.
   I have Geography on Mondays and Tuesdays in Sr. Beloso's classroom.

8. *¿En qué aula tenéis ciencias?*
    In which classroom do you have Science?
    Tengo ciencias en aula C104.
    I have Science in room C104.

Exercise 3.19
Pupil's Book: Page 68.

Pupils should use their own timetables when answering the questions that follow. Those using the CD Rom can display the meanings of the questions by clicking on the Union Flag icons.

1. When does your next Spanish lesson begin?
2. When does your next English lesson begin?
3. When does your next Maths lesson begin?
4. When does your next French lesson begin?
5. When does your next Sport lesson begin?
6. When does your next History lesson begin?

Exercise 3.20
Pupil's Book: Page 69.

1. What do you do at 9.00?
    I arrive at school.

2. What do you do at 10.00?
    I learn Spanish.

3. What do you do at 11.00?
    I have a break.

4. What do you (all) do at 1.00?
    We eat!

Those using the CD Rom can display the translations by clicking on the Union Flag icons. The distinction between *haces* and *hacéis* should be discussed, together with ways in which the difference could be brought out in a translation.

Exercise 3.21
Pupil's Book: Page 69.

Once pupils have translated the questions into Spanish they should then be encouraged to give answers, out loud or written, to the questions.

1. *¿Qué haces en la escuela los lunes?*
2. *¿Qué hacemos hoy después del almuerzo?*
3. *¿Qué hacéis en casa después de la escuela?*
4. *¿Qué hacen los profesores hoy a las tres y media?*
5. *¿Qué hacemos los viernes después del almuerzo?*

Those using the CD Rom can display the translations by clicking on the Spanish flag icons.

Exercise 3.22
Pupil's Book: Page 69.

This exercise gives more practice at answering question on the school routine. Those using the CD Rom can display the translations of the questions by clicking on the Union Flag icons.

1.   How many subjects do you study at school?
2.   How many subjects are compulsory?
3.   Which are the optional subjects?
4.   When do your lessons begin?
5.   Is there a break? When? What do you do during the break?
6.   When do you eat?
7.   Which is your favourite subject? Why?
8.   Which subject do you not like? Why?
9.   When does your school (day) end?
10.   Do you like your school? Why?

Exercise 3.23
Pupil's Book: Page 69.

This exercise gives extensive opportunity for writing about the school day, practising the use of the radical changing verbs covered in this unit.

Exercise 3.24
Pupil's Book: Page 70; CD 1, track: 78

In this exercise pupils read or listen to an account of a typical school day at a Spanish school for a pupil in Year 11. The audio track is read by a girl called Bea, and the pupil's book has an identical account written by a boy called Eduardo; it is assumed that, while most pupils will pick up on the fact that the names are different, this will not cause them any difficulty! They may also note that Bea does not pose the two final questions at the end of the passage (*¿Qué os parece mi horario? ¿Vosotros tenéis que trabajar tanto?* = What do you think of my timetable? Do you have to work as hard as me?)

Those using the CD Rom can display the answers to the questions (put to Bea!), by clicking on the **?** icons.

Track 78:

MI HORARIO

¡Hola! Soy Bea Hernández. Tengo dieciséis años y estoy en el 4º año de Educación Secundaria en la Academia Santa Teresa en Málaga.

Os voy a hablar sobre mi horario. Tengo clases desde las 8.15 hasta las 2.30, de lunes a viernes. Hay un recreo de media hora a las 12.30 en el que solemos tomar un bocadillo o un donut y charlar con los amigos. Cada clase dura 55 minutos – mucho, ¿verdad?

Estudio muchas asignaturas: tengo 4 clases de lengua española, matemáticas e inglés por semana; 3 clases de geografía, historia, física, química e informática. Tengo también 2 clases de ética, y una hora de religión, dibujo y educación física. Normalmente hacemos gimnasia pero a veces jugamos al balonmano, baloncesto y fútbol sala (5 personas por equipo). ¡Ah, se me olvidaba, una vez por semana tengo una hora de tutoría! Lo bueno es que no hay clases por la tarde pero lo malo es que hay deberes todos los días – ¡qué pesado!

Translation

Hi! I am Bea Hernández. I am 16 years old and I am in the 4th year of the secondary school at the Academia Santa Teresa in Málaga.

I am going to talk to you about my timetable. I have lessons from 8.15 until 2.30, Monday to Friday. There is a break of half an hour at 12.30 during which we usually eat a sandwich or a donut and chat with our friends. Each lesson lasts 55 minutes – that's a lot, isn't it?

I study many subjects: I have 4 lessons of Spanish language, Maths and English each week; 3 lessons of Geography, History, Physics, Chemistry and Information Technology. I also have 2 lessons of Ethics, and 1 lesson of Religious Studies, Art and Physical Education. Normally we do gym but sometimes we play handball, basketball and indoor football (5 a-side). Ah, I was forgetting, once a week I have a one hour tutorial. The good thing is that there are no lessons in the afternoon but the bad thing is that there is homework every day – what a pain!

Answers (Spanish/English):

1. Where does Eduardo study?
   Eduardo estudia en la Academia Santa Teresa en Málaga.
   Eduardo studies in the Academia Santa Teresa in Málaga.

2. Which year is he in?
   Está en 4º de ESO.
   He is in the fourth year of ESO.

3. When do the lessons begin and when do they end?
   Empiezan a las 8.15 y terminan a las 2.30.
   They begin at 8.15 and end at 2.30.

4. Does he have school on Saturdays?
   No tiene colegio los sábados.
   He does not have school on Saturdays.

5. When is break? And what do they do in break?
   Hay un recreo a las 12.30 en el que suelen tomar un bocadillo o un donut y charlar con los amigos.
   There is a break at 12.30 during which they usually eat a sandwich or a donut and chat with friends.

6. How long does each lesson last?
   Cada clase dura 55 minutos.
   Each lesson lasts for 55 minutes.

7. How many lessons a week does he have of English and Physics?
   Tiene 4 clases de inglés y 3 de física.
   He has four English lessons and three Physics.

8. Which sports does he do at school?
   Practica gimnasia, balonmano, baloncesto y fútbol sala.
   He does gymnastics, handball, basketball and indoor football.

9. What is the bad thing about his school?
   Lo malo es que hay deberes todos los días.
   The bad thing is that there is homework every day.

10. What is the good thing?
    Lo bueno es que no hay clases por la tarde.
    The good thing is that there are no lessons in the afternoon.

Exercise 3.25
Pupil's Book: Page 71.

Those using the CD Rom can display the full conjugation of each verb by clicking on the appropriate buttons.

1. *Practicar* = to practise

	Singular		**Plural**	
1st person	*practico*	I practise	*practicamos*	we practise
2nd person	*practicas*	you practise	*practicáis*	you practise
3rd person	*practica*	he/she/it practises	*practican*	they practise

2. *Escribir* = to write

	Singular		**Plural**	
1st person	*escribo*	I write	*escribimos*	we write
2nd person	*escribes*	you write	*escribís*	you write
3rd person	*escribe*	he/she/it writes	*escriben*	they write

3. *Comer* = to eat

	Singular		**Plural**	
1st person	*como*	I eat	*comemos*	we eat
2nd person	*comes*	you eat	*coméis*	you eat
3rd person	*come*	he/she/it eats	*comen*	they eat

4. *Tener* = to have

	Singular		**Plural**	
1st person	*tengo*	I have	*tenemos*	we have
2nd person	*tienes*	you have	*tenéis*	you have
3rd person	*tiene*	he/she/it has	*tienen*	they have

5. *Preferir (ie)* = to prefer

	Singular		**Plural**	
1st person	*prefiero*	I prefer	*preferimos*	we prefer
2nd person	*prefieres*	you prefer	*preferís*	you prefer
3rd person	*prefiere*	he/she/it prefers	*prefieren*	they prefer

6. *Pensar (ie)* = to think

	Singular		**Plural**	
1st person	*pienso*	I think	*pensamos*	we think
2nd person	*piensas*	you think	*pensáis*	you think
3rd person	*piensa*	he/she/it thinks	*piensan*	they think

7. *Vender* = to sell

	Singular		**Plural**	
1st person	*vendo*	I eat	*vendemos*	we eat
2nd person	*vendes*	you eat	*vendéis*	you eat
3rd person	*vende*	he/she/it eats	*venden*	they eat

8. *Decidir* = to decide

	Singular		**Plural**	
1st person	*decido*	I write	*decidimos*	we write
2nd person	*decides*	you write	*decidís*	you write
3rd person	*decide*	he/she/it writes	*deciden*	they write

9. **Escuchar** = *to listen*

	Singular		Plural	
1st person	escuch**o**	I listen	escuch**amos**	we listen
2nd person	escuch**as**	you listen	escuch**áis**	you listen
3rd person	escuch**a**	he/she/it listens	escuch**an**	they listen

10. **Ser** = **to be**

	Singular		Plural	
1st person	soy	I am	somos	we are
2nd person	eres	you are	sois	you are
3rd person	es	he/she/it is	son	they are

11. **Hacer** = *to do, make*

	Singular		Plural	
1st person	hago	I do	hacemos	we do
2nd person	haces	you do	hacéis	you do
3rd person	hace	he/she/it does	hacen	they do

12. **Hablar** = *to speak*

	Singular		Plural	
1st person	habl**o**	I speak	habl**amos**	we speak
2nd person	habl**as**	you speak	habl**áis**	you speak
3rd person	habl**a**	he/she/it speaks	habl**an**	they speak

La comida y la bebida
Pupil's Book: Page 72-3.

This brief look at food and drink gives an opportunity for those who have visited Spain to discuss the various meals they may have enjoyed there.

Exercise 3.26
Pupil's Book: Page 74; CD 1, tracks: 79-84

This long reading passage can also be listened to on the audio CD. After the first two paragraphs, the paragraphs are read as separate tracks to allow teachers to keep the passage down to a mangeagable length.

Track 79:

La familia Hernández es una típica familia española. Viven en Madrid.

Por la mañana, para desayunar, los señores Hernández normalmente beben café con leche, pero a sus tres hijos no les gusta. Pablo, el mayor, toma un vaso de leche caliente, mientras que sus hermanos menores, Eduardo y Mari Carmen, prefieren tomar Colacao. Los padres comen pan tostado con un poco de queso y jamón. Sus hijos prefieren galletas María, donuts o algunas veces un yogur. No suelen tomar cereales para el desayuno como en Inglaterra.

Track 80:

A las dos y pico, el señor Hernández vuelve a casa para comer porque trabaja cerca en una oficina. Su mujer es ama de casa y por eso prepara la comida para su familia. Pablo no regresa a casa para comer porque estudia en la Universidad. Eduardo y Mari Carmen sí vuelven para almorzar porque su colegio está cerca.

Track 81:

De primer plato casi siempre toman sopa (sobre todo en invierno) o una ensalada o verduras, o a veces una tortilla española.

Track 82:

De segundo comen carne – pollo con patatas fritas o filetes de ternera – o pescado – merluza, lenguado o mariscos. A veces la madre prepara un cocido muy sabroso con garbanzos – ¡el famoso cocido madrileño!, que les gusta mucho. Siempre comen pan con la comida y suelen beber agua mineral sin gas. Los padres toman también vino tinto o blanco. De postre normalmente toman fruta, flan o en verano algunas veces helado.

Track 83:

Después de la comida, sobre las 3, el señor Hernández tiene que volver a la oficina y sus dos hijos menores al colegio. A las 6 Eduardo y Mari Carmen regresan a casa (con bastante hambre) y toman la merienda – normalmente un vaso de Nesquik o leche con un bollo o pan con nocilla.

Track 84:

La cena empieza a eso de las 9 y consiste en algo más ligero que la comida – a veces una tortilla francesa, algo de pasta, o quizás un poco de pescado o verdura, queso o jamón. A la familia Hernández no les gusta cenar mucho de noche, porque no es sano.

Translation

The Hernández family is a typical Spanish family. They live in Madrid.

In the morning for breakfast, the Hernandez grown-ups normally drink white coffee, but the three children do not like it. Pablo, the oldest one, has a glass of hot milk, whereas his younger brothers, Eduardo and Mari Carmen, prefer to have Colacao. The parents eat toasted bread with a little cheese and ham. Their children prefer Maria biscuits, donuts or sometimes yoghurt. They don't usually have cereals for breakfast like in England.

Soon after two o'clock, Mr. Hernández returns home to eat because he works nearby in an office. His wife is a housewife and so she prepares the food for her family. Pablo does not return home to eat because he studies in the University. Eduardo and Mari Carmen do return to have lunch because their school is close.

For the first course they almost always have a soup (especially in winter) or a salad or vegetables, or sometimes a Spanish omelette.

For their second (course) they eat meat – chicken with chips or fillets of beef – or fish – hake, sole or seafood. Sometimes the mother prepares a very flavoursome Spanish stew with chick-peas – the famous Madrilenian Spanish stew, that they really like. They always eat bread with their food and they usually drink still mineral water. The parents also have red or white wine. For dessert they normally have fruit, creme caramel, or in summer sometimes ice-cream.

After the food, around 3.00, Mr. Hernández has to return to the office and his two younger children to the school. At 6.00 Eduardo and Mari Carmen return home (quite hungry) and have a snack: normally a glass of Nesquik or milk with a bun or bread with chocolate spread.

Supper begins about 9.00 and consists of something lighter than lunch; sometimes a French omelette, some pasta, or perhaps a little fish or vegetable, cheese or ham. The Hernández family do not like to eat much at night, because it is not healthy.

Ejercicio A

1. *La familia Hernández es una típica familia:*
    c) *española*
    The Hernández family is a typical **Spanish** family.

2. *Para el desayuno toman:*
    c) *café con leche, leche y Colacao*
    For breakfast they have **white coffee, milk and Colacao**.

3. *Los padres desayunan:*
    c) *tostadas*
    The parents have **toast** for breakfast.

4. *Comen a las dos:*
    b) *y pico*
    They eat **just after** 2.00.

Those using the CD Rom can display the answers by clicking on the **?** icons.

Ejercicio B

¿Verdad o mentira?

1. Mari Carmen prepares the lunch. (✗)
2. The whole family eats lunch at home. (✗)
3. For the first course they normally have soup or salad. (✓)
4. For the second course they only eat meat. (✗)
5. Cocido is a typical dish from Barcelona. (✗)
6. They all drink wine with lunch. (✗)

Ejercicio C

1.   *¿Cuál es el postre normalmente?*
        What is the dessert normally?

Answer: *Normalmente el postre es fruta, flan o helado.*
        Normally dessert is fruit, flan or ice-cream.

2.   *¿Qué comen siempre con la comida?*
        What do they always have with lunch?

Answer: *Siempre comen pan con la comida.*
        They always have bread with their lunch.

3.   *¿Qué beben?*
        What do they drink?

Answer: *Suelen beber agua mineral sin gas.*
        They usually drink still mineral water.

4.   *¿A qué hora meriendan Eduardo y Mari Carmen?*
        When do Eduardo and Mari Carmen have their snack?

Answer: *Eduardo y Mari Carmen toman la merienda a las 6.*
        Eduardo and Mari Carmen have their snack at 6.00.

5.   *¿Qué toman para la merienda?*
            What do they have for their snack?

Answer: *Normalmente toman un vaso de Nesquik o leche con un bollo o pan con nocilla..*
            They normally have a glass of Nesquik or milk with a bun or bread with chocolate spread.

6.   *¿Cuándo cenan?*
            When do they have dinner?

Answer: *La cena empieza sobre las 9.*
            Dinner begins at around 9.00.

7.   *¿En qué consiste la cena?*
            What does dinner consist of?

Answer: *La cena consiste de una tortilla, o pasta, o pescado, verduras, queso o jamón.*
            Dinner consists of an omlette, or pasta, or fish, vegetables, cheese or ham.

8.   *¿Por qué no cenan mucho?*
            Why do they not eat much?

Answer: *No cenan mucho porque no es sano.*
            They do not eat much because it is not healthy.

Exercise 3.27
Pupil's Book: Page 75.

This exercise gives practice at answering questions on food and mealtimes. Those using the CD Rom can see suggested answers to the questions as follows:

1.   *¿A qué hora desayunas?*
            When do you have breakfast?

Answer: *Desayuno a las siete.*
            I have breakfast at 7.00.

2.   *¿Qué tomas para el desayuno? ¿Qué bebes?*
            What do you have for breakfast?

Answer: *Normalmente tomo zumo de naranja y tostadas.*
            I normally have orange juice and toast.

3.   *¿Cuándo tomas el almuerzo?*
            When do you have lunch?

Answer: *Tomo el almuerzo a las dos.*
            I have lunch at 2.00.

4.   *¿Cuál es tu comida preferida?*
            What is your favourite meal?

Answer: *Mi comida preferida es pollo con patatas fritas.*
            My favourite meal is chicken and chips.

5.   *¿Cuál es tu bebida preferida?*
            What is your favourite drink?

Answer: *Mi bebida preferida es la cerveza.*
            My favourite drink is beer.

Exercise 3.28
Pupil's Book: Page 76; CD 1, track: 85

This long reading passage can be brought to life by allowing pupils to listen to the accompanying audio track.

Track 85:

José: *¡Hola! Cristina y yo hacemos una encuesta sobre la comida en nuestro colegio. Queremos saber cuántos alumnos comen en el cole, cuáles son sus comidas favoritas, qué beben normalmente, cuánto tiempo dura el almuerzo, y qué piensan de la comida.*

Cristina: *Sí, y también queremos saber qué comen en casa. Pensamos que todo el mundo debería tener una dieta equilibrada y queremos saber si las comidas en este colegio son sanas.*

José: *Empezamos con los alumnos más jóvenes de nuestro colegio. Éste es Juan...*

Cristina: *Y ésta es Teresa. Así que Teresa, ¿qué tal?*

Teresa: *Muy bien, gracias. ¿Y tú?*

Cristina: *Estupendo, gracias. Así que ¿cuál es la hora de comer?*

Teresa: *Sí, comemos a la una y media. Tenemos cuarenta y cinco minutos para el almuerzo.*

Cristina: *¿Qué tomas hoy, Juan?*

Juan: *Hoy tomo cocido con patatas y verduras. Bebo agua; ¡sólo hay agua en el cole!*

Cristina: *¿Cuál es tu comida favorita, Teresa?*

Teresa: *Mi comida favorita es la paella pero me gusta también el pescado y me encanta la pizza.*

Cristina: *Gracias, Teresa. Gracias, Juan. ¡Qué aproveche!*

Translation:

José: Hello. Cristina and I are conducting a survey about the food at our school. We want to know how many pupils eat in school, what their favourite food is, what they normally drink, how long lunch lasts and what they think of the food.

Cristina: Yes, and also we want to know what they eat at home. We think that everyone ought to have a balanced diet and we want to know if the lunches in this school are healthy.

José: We begin with the youngest pupils at our school. This is Juan.

Cristina: And this is Teresa. So Teresa, how are you?

Teresa: Very well, thanks. And you?

Cristina: Brilliant, thanks. So, what time is lunch?

Teresa: Yes, we eat at 1.30. We have 45 minutes for lunch.

Cristina: What do you have today, Juan?

Juan: Today I have stew with potatoes and vegetables. I drink water; there is only water in school.

Cristina: What is your favourite food, Teresa?

Teresa: My favourite food is paella but I also like fish and I love pizza.

Cristina: Thanks, Teresa. Thanks, Juan. Enjoy your meal!

Answers

1.   What type of survey is it?

Answer: *Es una encuesta sobre la comida en el colegio.*
It is a survey on the food at the school.

2.   Why is it important, according to Cristina?

Answer: *Es importante porque piensa que todo el mundo debería tener una dieta equilibrada.*
It is important because everyone ought to have a balanced diet.

3.   Who are the first pupils that José and Cristina interview?

Answer: *José y Cristina empiezan con los alumnos más jóvenes.*
José and Cristina begin with the youngest pupils.

4.   At what time do the pupils eat?

Answer: *Comen a la una y media.*
They eat at 1.30.

5.   How long do they have to eat?

Answer: *Tienen cuarenta y cinco minutos para el almuerzo.*
They have 45 minutes for lunch.

6.   Describe what Juan eats.

Answer: *Juan toma cocido con patatas y verduras.*
uan eats stew with potatoes and vegetables.

7.   What is Teresa's favourite food? And what are the other foods she mentions?

Answer: *La comida favorita de Teresa es la paella, pero a ella le gustan también el pescado y la pizza.*
Teresa'a favourtie food is paella, but she also likes fish and pizza.

8.   What does Cristina say at the end of the interview?

Answer: *Al final Cristina dice "¡que aproveche!"*
At the end Cristina says "enjoy your meal!"

Those using the CD Rom can display the answers to the questions by clicking on the **?** icons.

Exercise 3.29
Pupil's Book: Page 78; CD 1, track: 86

Again, this long reading passage can be brought to life by allowing pupils to listen to the accompanying audio track.

Track 86:

José: *Hola, Cristina y yo hacemos una encuesta en nuestro colegio. ¿Cómo te llamas?*

Eduardo: *Yo me llamo Eduardo. Soy nuevo en el colegio. Estoy en el segundo año de Educación Secundaria. Ésta es mi amiga Elena.*

José: *¿Qué piensas de la comida aquí?*

Eduardo: *¡Es horrible! y no hay suficiente para elegir.*

Elena: *El es muy especial para la comida. La comida está bien. A mí me chifla el cocido, y las pizzas, claro.*

José: *¿Cuál es tu comida favorita?*

Elena: *Es el cochinillo, pero no lo comemos nunca en el cole. Lo tomamos en casa y está riquísimo.*

José: *¿Y tú, Eduardo? ¿Qué comida te gusta más?*

Eduardo: *¿A mí? Pues, me gusta el pollo al ajillo y los calamares a la romana. Mi abuela los cocina muy bien el fin de semana. ¡Es una cocinera fantástica!*

Translation:

José: Hello, Cristina and I are doing a survey at our school. What is your name?

Eduardo: My name is Eduardo. I am new at the school. I am in the 2nd year of ESO. This is my friend Elena.

José: What do you think of the food here?

Eduardo: It's horrible! There is not enough to choose from.

Elena: He is very fussy about food. The food is good. I love the stew, and the pizzas of course.

José: What is your favourite food?

Elena: It is the suckling pig, but we don't have that now at school. We have it at home and it is delicious.

José: And you, Eduardo? Which food do you like best?

Eduardo: Me? Well, I like chicken cooked in garlic and squid in batter. My grandmother cooks these very well at the weekend. She is a fantastic cook!

Questions:

1.   Who is Eduardo? And which class is he in?

Answer: *Eduardo es un alumno nuevo en el colegio. Está en el segundo año de Educación Secundaria.*
Eduardo is a new pupil at the school. He is in the 2nd year of secondary school.

2.   Who is Elena?

Answer: *Elena es una amiga de Eduardo.*
Elena is a friend of Eduardo.

3.   What does Eduardo think of the food at school?

Answer: *Eduardo piensa que la comida es horrible.*
Eduardo thinks that the food is horrible.

4.   Why does he think that?

Answer: *Eduardo es muy especial para la comida y piensa que no hay suficiente para elegir.*
Eduardo is very fussy about food and thinks that there is not enough choice.

5.   Does Elena share Eduardo's opinion?

Answer: *No, Elena piensa que Eduardo es muy especial para la comida. A ella le gusta la comida.*
No, Elena thinks that Eduardo is very fussy about the food. She likes the food.

6.   Which school foods does Elena mention?

Answer: *Elena menciona el cocido y las pizzas.*
Elena mentions the stew and the pizzas.

7.   Which is her favourite food? Where does she eat it?

Answer: *La comida preferida de Elena es cochinillo. Lo toma en casa.*
Elena's favourite food is suckling pig. She eats it at home.

8.   What is Eduardo's favourite food? And who prepares it for him?

Answer: *La comida preferida de Eduardo es el pollo al ajillo y los calamares a la romana. Su abuela los cocina.*
Eduardo's favourite food is chicken cooked in garlic or squid in batter. His grandmother cooks them.

UNIT 4: En casa

In this unit pupils learn to ask questions about daily routines and where they live. They describe what they and others do and begin to develop creative writing skills.

Where the unit fits in

This unit extends pupils' knowledge and experience of how to reuse and adapt previously learnt language in the new context of the home. Pupils increase their vocabulary and start to work more independently by using a simple glossary.

New contexts:

- daily routine
- simple descriptions of homes

New language content:

- reflexive verbs
- radical changing verbs o ue
- both verbs meaning 'to be': ser and estar
- numbers above 100
- ordinal numbers
- prepositions

Expectations

At the end of this unit most pupils will: understand and use reflexive verbs to describe and ask questions about daily routines; talk and write about their home and what they do at home; understand and use numbers greater than 100 and give an address in Spanish; describe a room, orally and in writing, saying where items of furniture are.

Some pupils will not have made so much progress and will: understand familiar statements about where people live and what they do; give simple responses to questions about where they live and what they do at home; describe a room, using visuals and labels as prompts.

Some pupils will have progressed further and will: understand a more detailed written or spoken text about where people live; memorise and use vocabulary and all persons of verbs; use a glossary or dictionary effectively.

N.B. The audio tracks for Units 4-6 are on the second audio CD.

Exercise 4.1
Pupil's Book: Page 82.

1. *Dormimos en la clase.*
2. *Almuerzan a la una.*
3. *Vuelvo del colegio a las cuatro y media.*
4. *Mis amigos y yo almorzamos en la cantina.*
5. *Mi profesor vuelve a Extremadura cada año.*
6. *Duermo hasta las once los domingos.*

Those using the CD Rom can display the translations by clicking on the Spanish flag icons.

Exercise 4.2
Pupil's Book: Page 82.

1. *Soler (ue)*

suelo	*solemos*
sueles	*soléis*
suele	*suelen*

2. *Jugar (ue)*

juego	*jugamos*
juegas	*jugáis*
juega	*juegan*

3. *Encontrar (ue)*

encuentro	*encontramos*
encuentras	*encontráis*
encuentra	*encuentran*

4. *Torcer (ue)*

tuerco	*torcemos*
tuerces	*torcéis*
tuerce	*tuercen*

Those using the CD Rom can display the answers by clicking on the **?** icons.

Exercise 4.3
Pupil's Book: Page 83.

1. (a)

Me levanto	*Nos levantamos*
Te levantas	*Os levantáis*
Se levanta	*Se levantan*

(b)

Me baño	*Nos bañamos*
Te bañas	*Os bañáis*
Se baña	*Se bañan*

(c)

Me lavo	*Nos lavamos*
Te lavas	*Os laváis*
Se lava	*Se lavan*

(d)

Me ducho	*Nos duchamos*
Te duchas	*Os ducháis*
Se ducha	*Se duchan*

Those using the CD Rom can display the answers by clicking on the **?** icons.

Exercise 4.4
Pupil's Book: Page 84; Audio CD 2 track: 1
Audio CD 2 track 1:

Me llamo Juan y me despierto a las siete. Me levanto normalmente a las siete y media. Después de levantarme, me ducho en el cuarto de baño. Después de vestirme, tomo el desayuno en el comedor. Mi hermana se levanta a las siete. No se ducha normalmente pero se lava el pelo cada mañana. Mis padres son muy perezosos ¡Siempre se levantan a las ocho y media! Por la tarde me acuesto bastante tarde, a las once y media.

Answers

1.	*Juan se levanta **a las siete y media** (i).*	Juan gets up at 7.30.
2.	*Se ducha en el cuarto de baño (g).*	He has a shower in the bathroom.
3.	*Su hermana se levanta **a las siete** (f).*	His sister gets up at 7.00.
4.	*Se lava el pelo **cada mañana** (e).*	She washes her hair every morning.
5.	*Los padres de Juan se levantan **a las ocho y media** (b).*	Juan's parents get up at 8.30.
6.	*Juan se acuesta **a las once y media** (d).*	Juan goes to bed at 11.30.

Those using the CD Rom can display the phrases 1-6 on the screen, and pupils drag the answers (a) – (i) onto the correct phrases.

Exercise 4.5
Pupil's Book: Page 84.

In this screen, clicking on the ? icon reveals the correct translation.

1. I normally get up at 10.00.
2. His friends are called Pedro and Juan.
3. We get up late on Sundays.
4. My brother doesn't wash!
5. You brush your teeth in the bathroom.

Those using the CD Rom can display the translations by clicking on the Union Flag icons.

Exercise 4.6
Pupil's Book: Page 84.

1. *Me ducho cada mañana.*
2. *Me lavo el pelo los martes y los viernes.*
3. *Se despierta a las seis y media.*
4. *Se quitan la ropa en su dormitorio.*
5. *Vds. se acuestan bastante tarde.*

Those using the CD Rom can display the translations by clicking on the Spanish flag icons.

Exercise 4.7
Pupil's Book: Page 85; Audio CD 2 track: 2

In this exercise, we hear Julián describing his day.

Audio CD 2 track 2:

Hola, me llamo Julián y me levanto cada mañana a las siete. Me levanto y me ducho en el cuarto de baño. Después, me visto en el dormitorio y arreglo las cosas antes de tomar el desayuno. Suelo tomar cereales, un zumo de naranja y un café. No me gustan ni el té ni el café con leche. Después de desayunar, me lavo los dientes y salgo de casa para coger el metro para llegar al instituto. Hay una parada cerca de mi casa y el viaje dura 10 minutos. Almuerzo en la cantina del colegio y hago los deberes por la tarde. Normalmente vuelvo a mi casa a las 6.

Corrections:

1.	*Julián se levanta a las siete.*	Julián gets up at 7.00.
2.	*Se ducha en el cuarto de baño.*	He has a shower in the bathroom.
3.	*Se viste antes de tomar el desayuno.*	He gets dressed before having breakfast.
4.	*Le gusta el café solo.*	He likes black coffee.
5.	*Se lava los dientes después de tomar el desayuno.*	He brushes his teeth after having breakfast.
6.	*Coge el metro para llegar al instituto.*	He takes the subway to get to the school.
7.	*El viaje dura 10 minutos.*	The journey lasts ten minutes.
8.	*Almuerza en la cantina del colegio.*	He has lunch in the school canteen.
9.	*Hace sus deberes por la tarde.*	He does his homework in the afternoon.
10.	*Vuelve a su casa a las seis.*	He returns home at 6.00.

Those using the CD Rom can display the corrections by clicking on the ? icons.

Exercise 4.8
Pupil's Book: Page 85.

This exercise allows pupils to practise asking and answering questions on daily routine. Those using the CD Rom hear the questions being posed in Spanish. Clicking on the Union Flag icons reveal the English. Suggested answers have not been given, as each pupil will have different answers to give.

1. When do you wake up in the morning?
2. When do you get dressed?
3. Do you have a shower or a bath in the morning?
4. What do you do after getting dressed?
5. What do you have for breakfast?
6. What do you do before leaving to go to school?

Exercise 4.9
Pupil's Book: Page 86; Audio CD 2 track: 3

In this exercise we hear about Antonio's typical working day at the Academia Santa Teresa in Málaga.

Audio CD 2 track 3

Un día en la vida de un conserje de colegio

ANTONIO trabaja como conserje en la Academia Santa Teresa en Málaga. Es un colegio mixto y privado.

Suele levantarse bastante temprano: sobre las seis y media de la mañana. Primero se ducha y luego se viste. No le gusta desayunar mucho así que sólo toma un café con leche.

Su casa está a veinte minutos del colegio en coche. Suele llegar a las ocho menos cuarto – ¡llega siempre el primero! Abre el colegio: es decir, la cancela, las clases, el laboratorio, la biblioteca, la sala de profesores y la capilla.

Sobre las diez suele tomar un bocadillo y un café. Durante el día es responsable del mantenimiento del colegio: arregla las puertas, las pizarras, las cerraduras, las luces, los proyectores etc. y si hay algún problema intenta solucionarlo. ¡Hace muchas "chapuzas"!

Su día laboral termina a las tres de la tarde cuando va a su casa y no vuelve hasta el día siguiente. Trabaja de lunes a sábado pero los sábados empieza a las nueve, y ¡qué suerte ese día! no hay clases, no hay niños ......

Translation:

Antonio works as a caretaker in the Academia Santa Teresa in Málaga. It is a mixed, private school.

He usually gets up quite early: around 6.30 in the morning. First he has a shower and then he gets dressed. He doesn't like much for breakfast, so he just has a white coffee.

His house is 20 minutes from the school by car. He usually arrives at 7.45 – he is always the first to arrive! He opens up the school; that is to say the gate, the classrooms, the laboratory, the library, the staffroom and the chapel.

Around 10.00 he usually has a sandwich and a cup of coffee. During the day he is responsible for the maintenance of the school: he fixes the doors, the windows, the whiteboards, the locks, the lights, the projectors etc. and if there is any problem, he tries to solve it. He does lots of odd jobs!

His working day finishes a 3.00 in the afternoon when he goes home and does not return until the following day. He works from Monday to Saturday but on Saturdays he begins at 9.00 and what a lucky day! There are no lessons and no children…

Answers:

1. When does Antonio normally get up?
   Suele levantarse sobre las seis y media.
   He normally gets up at around 6.30.

2. What does he have for breakfast?
   Sólo toma un café con leche para desayunar.
   He just has a cup of white coffee for breakfast.

3. Does he live far from the school?
   Vive a veinte minutos del colegio en coche.
   He lives 20 minutes from the school by car.

4. When does he arrive at the school?
   Suele llegar al colegio a las ocho menos cuarto.
   He usually arrives at the school at 7.45.

5. What does he do when he arrives?
   Cuando llega, abre el colegio.
   When he arrives he opens up the school.

6. What does he do at around 10.00?
   Sobre las diez suele tomar un bocadillo y un café.
   At around 10.00 he usually has a sandwich and a cup of coffee.

7. What is his work like during the day?
   Durante el día es responsable del mantenimiento del colegio.
   During the day he is responsible for the maintenance of the school.

8.   When does his day at the school finish?
     Su día en el colegio termina a las tres de la tarde.
     His day at the school finishes at 3.00 in the afternoon.

9.   How many days does he work during the week?
     Trabaja de lunes a sábado.
     He works from Monday to Saturday.

10. Why does he prefer to work on Saturdays?
     Prefiere trabajar los sábados porque no hay niños.
     He prefers working on Saturdays because there are no children.

Exercise 4.10
Pupil's Book: Page 87.

1.   *Suelo levantarme a las siete y media.*

2.   *Sueles lavarte antes de desayunar.*

3.   *Suele escuchar su compact disc de camino al colegio.*

4.   *No solemos hablar mucho en el autobús.*

5.   *Sueles acostarte a las diez.*

6.   *Suelen ducharse bastante temprano los lunes.*

Exercise 4.11
Pupil's Book: Page 87.

Dear friend! How are you? I write about my family and my daily routine. Well, there are four of us in our family: my father, my mother, my sister and I. My father is 36 years old and is a doctor. He works in a hospital in the centre of Granada. My mother, who is Argentinian, is his secretary. The two of them work together in the same hospital. My older sister studies at the University of Granada but still live in our house. She is very nice and I get on well with her. I am 14 years old and I study at the San Diego school here in Granada. I am thin but very sporty. I usually wake up very early because I go swimming before breakfast. I normally get up at 5.15. After breakfast I have a shower and get dressed. I come back at 6.30, we have dinner at 9.00 and I normally go to bed at 10.45.
With best wishes, from Roberto.

Answers:

1.   *Hay cuatro personas **en su familia** (e).*   There are 4 people in his family.

2.   *Sus padres **trabajan juntos** (a).*   His parents work together.

3.   *Su madre **es de Argentina** (l).*   His mother is from Argentina.

4.   *Roberto y su hermana **estudian en Granada** (c).*   Roberto and his sister study in Granada.

5.   *Roberto **se ducha después de nadar** (i).*   Roberto has a shower after swimming.

6.   *Se acuesta **a las 10.45** (k).*   He goes to bed at 10.45.

Those using the CD Rom can drag the phrases (a)-(l) onto the correct phrases 1-6.

Exercise 4.12
Pupil's Book: Page 88; Audio CD 2 tracks: 4-8
Audio CD 2 track 4:

1.   *Me llamo Alfonso. Me despierto a las seis y media y me lavo en seguida.*
        My name is Alfonso. I wake up at 6.30 and I wash at once.

Audio CD 2 track 5:

2.   *Soy Laura. Me visto en mi dormitorio y luego desayuno.*
        I am Laura. I get dressed in my bedroom and then I have breakfast.

Audio CD 2 track 6:

3.   *¡Hola! Soy Miguel. Me levanto a las siete durante la semana pero los fines de semana, ¡me levanto a las once!*
        Hello! I am Miguel. I get up at 7.00 during the week but at the week-ends I get up at 11.00!

Audio CD 2 track 7:

4.   *Soy Victoria. Después de desayunar, me ducho.*
        I am Victoria. After breakfast, I have a shower.

Audio CD 2 track 8:

5.   *Me llamo Luis. Los fines de semana, me acuesto a los dos de la madrugada.*
        My name is Luis. At the week-ends I go to bed at 2.00 in the morning.

Answers:

1.   Alfonso wakes up at 7.30: False
2.   Alfonso has a shower after waking up: true.
3.   Laura gets dressed before breakfast: true.
4.   Miguel always gets up at 7.00: false.
5.   Victoria has a shower before breakfast: false.
6.   At the week-ends, Luis goes to bed very late: true.

Exercise 4.13
Pupil's Book: Page 88.

This exercise allows pupils to practise answering questions on their daily routine. Those using the CD Rom can listen to examples of the sort of answers they may wish to give to the questions.

1.   **Prof:** *¿A qué hora te despiertas por la mañana?*   When do you wake up in the morning?
        Juan: *Suelo despertarme a las siete.*   I normally wake up at 7.00.

2.   **Prof:** *¿A qué hora te levantas?*   When do you get up?
        Juan: *Suelo levantarme a las siete y media.*   I normally get up at 7.30.

3.   **Prof:** *¿Dónde te lavas?*   Where do you wash?
        Juan: *Suelo lavarme en el cuarto de baño.*   I normally wash in the bathroom.

4.   **Prof:** *¿Te duchas?*   Do you have a shower?
        Juan: *Suelo ducharme cada mañana.*   I normally have a shower every morning.

5.   **Prof:** *¿Dónde te vistes?*   Where do you get dressed?
        Juan: *Suelo vestirme en mi dormitorio.*   I usually get dressed in my bedroom.

| 6. | **Prof:** | ¿Dónde desayunas? | Where do you have breakfast? |
| | **Juan:** | Suelo tomar el desayuno en la cocina. | I usually have breakfast in the kitchen. |

| 7. | **Prof:** | ¿A qué hora te acuestas durante la semana? | When do you go to bed during the week? |
| | **Juan:** | Durante la semana suelo acostarme a las 10.00. | During the week I usually go to bed at 10.00. |

| 8. | **Prof:** | ¿A qué hora te acuestas los fines de semana? | When do you go to bed at the week-ends? |
| | **Juan:** | Los fines de semana suelo acostarme a las 11.30. | At the week-ends I usually go to bed at 11.30. |

Exercise 4.14
Pupil's Book: Page 88.

This exercise allows pupils to practise manipulating the language from the 3rd person to the 1st person. Those using the CD Rom can see and hear both the 3rd person version and a revised 1st person version.

Translation:

Miguel normally wakes up at 7.30. He gets up ten minutes later. He washes, he gets dressed and then he has breakfast: normally a white coffee and toast. He studies at school from 9.00 until 2.00. Then he eats at home. In the afternoon he watches the television, has supper and goes to bed at 10.00.

1st person singular version:

Me llamo Carolina. Suelo despertarme a las siete y media. Me levanto diez minutos después. Me lavo, me visto y luego desayuno: normalmente un café con leche y tostadas. Estudio en el colegio de 9 a 2. Luego como en casa. Por la tarde veo la televisión, ceno y me acuesto a las diez.

Exercise 4.15
Pupil's Book: Page 89.
Suggested answers:

07.15:	A las siete y cuarto mi hermana Bea se levanta y se lava los dientes.
07.30:	A las siete y media desayuna.
09.00:	A las nueve va al colegio.
15.30:	A las tres y media va de compras con su madre.
16.30:	A las cuatro y media sale con su hermana mayor.
16.45:	A las cinco menos cuarto va a una fiesta.
17.30:	A las cinco y media juega con su amiga en el jardín.
18.45:	A las siete menos cuarto su padre cocina en el jardín para toda la familia.
20.30:	A las ocho y media se acuesta.

Those using the CD Rom can click on each image to see the suggested answer (as above).

Vocabulario 4.1
Pupil's Book: Page 90.

Those using the CD Rom can display the vocabulary on the screen.

Estar
Pupil's Book: Page 90.

Those using the CD Rom can display the information on estar and the two examples on the screen.

Prepositions
Pupil's Book: Page 91.

Those using the CD Rom can display the information on prepositions, with pictures to illustrate the meaning of each one.

Exercise 4.16
Pupil's Book: Page 91.

Suggested answers:

1. *El padre está al lado del chico.*
2. *Los niños están al lado de los padres.*
3. *La madre está enfrente del chico.*
4. *La abuela está delante del abuelo.*
5. *El abuelo está detrás de la abuela.*

Those using the CD Rom can display the suggested answers by clicking on the **?** icons.

Exercise 4.17
Pupil's Book: Page 92-3; Audio CD 2 track: 9

Audio CD 2 Track 9:

Me llamo Joaquín. Vivo en un piso; está en el centro de Barcelona. Es un piso grande y cómodo.
Yo me llamo Charo. Vivo en un chalet moderno; está en la sierra, cerca de Madrid.
Me llamo Josefina. Vivo en una casa en el campo en las afueras de Santiago de Compostela.
Me llamo Basilio. Vivo en Colombia en una chabola.
Me llamo Alfredo. Vivo en una granja pequeña en Costa Rica.

Translation:

My name is Joaquín. I live in a flat; it is in the centre of Barcelona. It is a big, comfortable flat.
My name is Charo. I live in a modern chalet; it is in the mountains, near Madrid.
My name is Josefina. I live in a house in the country on the outskirts of Santiago de Compostela.
My name is Basilio. I live in Colombia in a shack.
My name is Alfredo. I live on a small farm in Costa Rica.

Answers:

1. *Joaquín vive en Barcelona.*
2. *Su piso es grande y cómodo.*
3. *Charo vive en un chalet.*
4. *El chalet es cerca de Madrid.*
5. *El chalet es moderno.*
6. *Josefina vive en las afueras de Santiago de Compostela.*
7. *No, Josefina vive en el campo.*
8. *Basilio vive en Colombia.*
9. *No, Basilio vive en una chabola.*
10. *No, Alfredo vive en una granja.*
11. *Su granja está en Costa Rica.*
12. *Su granja es pequeña.*

Those using the CD Rom can drag the correct answers onto the appropriate questions.

Exercise 4.18
Pupil's Book: Page 93.

This exercise gives pupils the opportunity to describe their own houses.

Exercise 4.19
Pupil's Book: Page 94.

1.   ¿Quién es? Es mi profesor – es francés.
2.   ¿Quiénes son? Son mis padres.
3.   ¿Cómo son? Son muy simpáticos.
4.   ¿Quién eres? Soy Paquita y soy española.
5.   ¿Quién eres? Soy Alfredo y soy argentino.
6.   ¿Cómo es tu abuela?
7.   ¿De qué nacionalidad eres?
8.   Somos alemanes.
9.   Usted es profesor, ¿verdad?
10. ¿Cómo son tus alumnos?
11. ¿Qué es?
12. ¿Cómo eres?

Those using the CD Rom can display the answers by clicking on the Spanish flag icons.

Exercise 4.20
Pupil's Book: Page 94.

1.   ¿Dónde está Madrid? Está en el centro de España.
2.   ¿Dónde están los chicos? Están en el colegio.
3.   ¿Dónde estás? Yo estoy en casa.
4.   ¿Dónde está usted? Yo estoy en la clase.
5.   ¿Dónde estáis?, Luis y Juan.
6.   Estamos en la plaza.
7.   ¿Dónde está tu casa?
8.   Está cerca de la estación.
9.   ¿Dónde está tu hermana?
10. ¿Está en la universidad.
11. ¿Cómo estás hoy? Yo estoy regular, gracias.
12   ¿Cómo está tu padre, hoy? Está muy bien.

Those using the CD Rom can display the answers by clicking on the Spanish flag icons.

Exercise 4.21
Pupil's Book: Page 95.

In this exercise pupils have to select the correct form of *ser* or *estar* (shown in bold) and should then translate.

1.   Mi padre **es** galés.   My father is Welsh.
2.   Mi casa **está** en Londres.   My house is in London.
3.   ¿Cómo **son** tus hermanos?   What are your brothers like?
4.   Mis abuelos **están** en el jardín.   My grandparents are in the garden.
5.   Nosotros **estamos** en el colegio.   We are in the school.
6.   Tú **eres** español; ¿verdad?   You are Spanish, aren't you?
7.   Yo **soy** alumna.   I am a pupil.

8.	*Usted **es** profesor.*	You are a teacher.
9.	*¿Dónde **está** usted?*	Where are you?
10.	*Mamá, yo **estoy** en el cuarto de baño.*	Mama, I am in the bathroom.
11.	*Tus amigos **son** muy simpáticos.*	Your friends are very nice.
12.	*¡Vosotros **estáis** muy pesados hoy!*	You are very boring today!

Those using the CD Rom can display the answers by clicking on the ? icons.

Exercise 4.22
Pupil's Book: Page 95.

In this exercise pupils practise answering a range of questions about their school and home.

Exercise 4.23
Pupil's Book: Page 95.

1. My mother is in the bathroom.
2. My animals are in the garden.
3. We are at school.
4. The uncle and aunt are in Sevilla.
5. The children are in their bedroom.

Those using the CD Rom can display the answers by clicking on the Union Flag icons.

Exercise 4.24
Pupil's Book: Page 95.

This screen allows pupils to see the correct translations of the following sentences:

1. *La chica está en su dormitorio.*
2. *Los chicos están en el jardín.*
3. *Mi padre está en el cuarto de baño.*
4. *Mis abuelos están en la cocina.*
5. *Su perro está en el vestíbulo.*

Those using the CD Rom can display the answers by clicking on the Spanish flag icons.

Exercise 4.25
Pupil's Book: Page 96; Audio CD 2 track: 10

This exercise allows pupils to explore the story of Santa Barbara.

Audio CD 2 Track 10:

Santa Bárbara es patrona de las armas de artillería y de los trabajadores de minas y explosivos. El día de Santa Bárbara se celebra el 2 de diciembre.

Según una vieja tradición, Santa Bárbara era hija de un hombre muy rudo llamado Dióscoro.

Ella no cree en los ídolos paganos de su padre, por lo que él la encierra en un castillo con dos ventanas pero ella manda añadir una tercera ventana para acordarse de las Tres Divinas Personas de la Santísima Trinidad. Por esto su padre se pone furioso y permite que la martiricen: le cortan la cabeza con una espada.

Así Santa Bárbara es representada con una espada y una corona porque es una mártir. La misma tradición dice que a su padre le cae un rayo y lo mata. Por este motivo, muchas personas rezan a la Santa para pedir protección contra los rayos de las tormentas.

Saint Bárbara is the patron saint of artillery weapons and of mines and explosives workers. The festival of Santa Bárbara is 2nd December. According to ancient tradition, Santa Bárbara is the daughter of a very coarse man called Dióscoro. She does not believe in the pagan idols of her father, and so he shuts her up in a castle with two windows but she orders a third to be added in memory of the Three Divinities of the Holy Trinity. For that her father grows angry and allows her to be tortured: he cuts off her head with a spade. So Santa Bárbara is represented with a spade and a crown because she becomes a martyr. The same tradition says that lightning strikes her father and kills him. For that reason, many people pray to the saint asking for protection against lightning and storms.

Answers:
1. *Santa Bárbara es santa de las armas de artillería y de los trabajadores de minas y explosivos.*
2. *El día de Santa Bárbara se celebra el 2 de diciembre.*
3. *El padre de Santa Bárbara se llama Dióscoro.*
4. *Dióscoro es un hombre muy rudo.*
5. *Su padre la encierra en un castillo porque ella no cree en los ídolos paganos.*
6. *El castillo tiene dos ventanas pero ella manda añadir una tercera.*
7. *Le cortan la cabeza con una espada.*
8. *A su padre le cae un rayo y lo mata.*

Those using the CD Rom can display the answers by clicking on the ? icons.

Exercise 4.26
Pupil's Book: Page 98.
Foreign addres formats are something of a mine-field, and this exercise is intended to help. Pupils could be encouraged to bring in their own Spanish addresses (perhaps of pen pals or foreign exchange students).

Suggested answers:
1. Sr. Beloso Domínguez lives in Flat A of building 22 in a street called Jose Clara, in Vilafortuny, in the region of Tarragona.
2. Sra. Palacín Melero lives in Flat A, on the 5th floor of building number 5 in the Vía Roma in Salou.
3. Sr. Santiago del Amo Rodríguez lives in Flat B on the 4th floor of building number 14 in a street called Martínez Maldonado in Málaga.
4. Sra. Lily Blanco lives in Costa Rica. Her address is a PO Box number, but we know that she lives in Moravia, near San José.
5. Snra. Haro Gutiérrez lives in Flat D on the 7th floor of number 34 in a street called Cáceres in Alcorcón, in the region of Madrid.

Exercise 4.27
Pupil's Book: Page 98; Audio CD 2 tracks: 11-16
In this exercise, pupils listen to the characters give details of where they live. They then transfer this information into address book format, using what they learnt above.

Audio track 11:
1. *Hola, soy Leticia y mi dirección es Avenida Gran Vía, número 24, planta tercera – B. Mi código postal es 43-0-41 y claro que vivo en Salou.*

Audio track 12:

2. *¿Qué hay? Soy Ignacio y soy de Madrid. ¿Mi piso? Bueno, se encuentra en la calle Toledo, 176, 4° D y mi código postal es el 28764.*

Audio track 13:

3. *Me llamo Helena y vivo cerca de Tarragona. Mi piso está situado en la 3ª planta D. El número es el 35 y el código postal es el 43878. La calle se llama Florida.*

Audio track 14:

4. *¡Saludos desde Costa Rica! Me llamo Luis y vivo cerca de Moravia. Vivo en Avenida Abel Pacheco, en un chalet cuyo número es el 56. ¿Mi código postal.....? Sí, es el 2179.*

Audio track 15:

5. *Hola, me llamo Francisco. Mi código postal es el 28243 y soy de Madrid. Vivo en la cuarta planta A, en un piso que está situado en la calle General Bernabeu, muy cerca del estadio de fútbol del Real Madrid. El número es el 48.*

Audio track 16:

6. *Hola me llamo Ann y vivo en St.Helens. Mi casa es bastante grande y su número es el 123. La calle se llama Ormskirk Road y el código postal es WA9 1BQ. Adiós y ¡qué lo pases muy bien!*

Answers:

1. Leticia
    Avenida Gran Vía
    24 – 3° – B
    43041 Salou
    ESPAÑA

2. Ignacio
    C/ Toledo 176 – 4° D
    28764 Madrid
    ESPAÑA

3. Helena
    C/ Florida 35 – 3°D
    43878 Tarragona
    ESPAÑA

4. Luis
    Avenida Abel Pacheco 56
    2179 Moravia
    COSTA RICA

5. Francisco
    c/ General Bernabeu 48-4°
    28243 Madrid
    ESPAÑA

6. Ann
    123 Ormskirk Road
    St Helens
    WA9 1BQ
    INGLATERRA

Exercise 4.28
Pupil's Book: Page 99.

This exercise provides further practice with prepositions as well as the rooms of the house.

1. *El padre está en el jardín.*
2. *La madre está detrás del padre.*
3. *El chico está al lado del padre.*
4. *La chica está sobre la cama.*
5. *El perro está en el salón.*
6. *El gato está en el jardín.*

Those using the CD Rom can drag the characters to different locations, allowing pupils to practise varying their answers each time the exercise is done.

Exercise 4.29
Pupil's Book: Page 99; Audio CD 2 track: 17

In this exercise, pupils hear Maribel tell where she and various members of her family are. They then fill the gaps and should then translate into English. We apologise for the whereabouts of the grandfather, but it does give practice at the pronunciation of the letter w!

Audio CD 2 track 17

Soy Maribel y estoy en el jardín. Mi hermano Francisco está en su dormitorio y mis padres están en el salón. ¡Mi abuelo, Victor, está sentado en el wáter!

I am Maribel and I am in the garden. My brother Francisco is in his bedroom and my parents are in the sitting-room. My grandfather, Victor, is sitting on the lavatory.

1. *Los padres de Maribel están en **el salón.***
   Maribel's parents are in the sitting room.

2. *Su hermano, que se llama Francisco está en **el dormitorio.***
   Her brother, who is called Francisco, is in the bedroom.

3. *Su abuelo está sentado en **el wáter**.*
   His grandfather is sitting on the lavatory.

4. *Maribel está en **el jardín**.*
   Maribel is in the garden.

Exercise 4.30
Pupil's Book: Page 100.

In this exercise, pupils look at the picture of the sitting room and answer the questions. A range of answers will be acceptable, depending on how specific pupils wish to be.

1. Where are the armchairs?
2. Where is the sofa?
3. Where is the lamp?
4. Where is the television?
5. Where is the video?
6. Where is the computer?

Exercise 4.31
Pupil's Book: Page 100; Audio CD 2 track: 18

In this exercise, Paco is lying on the sofa in the sitting room, talking to his mother who wants him to do his homework. Pupils use it as a model for a dialogue of their own with their partners. It should be noted that on the audio CD the mother uses the word *vago* rather than *pesado* (as printed in the pupil's book) in the final speech.

Audio CD 2 Track 18:

Madre:	*Oye, Paco, ¿dónde estás?*
Paco:	*Estoy aquí, mamá, en el sofá en la sala de estar.*
Madre:	*¿Qué haces?*
Paco:	*Hay un buen programa en la tele así que...*
Madre:	*Pero tienes muchos deberes, no?*
Paco:	*Sí, mamá pero prefiero ver mi programa favorito o jugar con el ordenador...*
Madre:	*Pero ¡Qué vago eres, hijo!*

Translation:

Madre:	Hey, Paco, where are you?
Paco:	I am here, mama, on the sofa in the sitting-room.
Madre:	What are you doing?
Paco:	There is a good programme on the T.V., so...
Madre:	But you have lots of homework, don't you?
Paco:	Yes, mama, but I prefer watching my favourite programme or playing on the computer...
Madre:	But how lazy you are, son!

Exercise 4.32
Pupil's Book: Page 101.

In this exercise, Paco is describing his bedroom. Pupils should first translate the passage. Then they cover the Spanish and try to describe the bedroom to their partners. Their partners can prompt them by asking questions.

Translation:

It is quite a large room with walls painted light blue. There are lots of posters. Near the window there is a bed and next to it a bedside table with a very modern lamp. On the left-hand side, in front of the door, there is a wardrobe and on the left a bookcase with lots of books. On the floor there is a little multi-coloured carpet.

La cocina
Pupil's Book: Page 102.

This screen shows the picture of the kitchen from the pupil's book, with the various items marked.

Exercise 4.33
Pupil's Book: Page 102-3; Audio CD 2 track: 19
Audio CD 2 Track 19:

A las 9, la señora Trujillo lava los platos del desayuno en el fregadero.
A las 10 pone la lavadora y después tiende la ropa.
Cinco minutos después friega el suelo.
Sobre las 12.30 empieza a preparar la comida. Saca el pescado y las verduras de la nevera.
Media hora después mete el pescado en el horno y cuece las verduras.
A las 2 en punto lleva la comida a la mesa del comedor.
Después de comer prepara un café para su marido.
Sobre las 3.30 pone los platos sucios en el lavaplatos.

Translation:

At 9.00 Mrs Trujillo washes the plates from breakfast in the sink.
At 10.00 she puts on the washing-machine and afterwards hangs up the washing.
Five minutes later she washes the floor.
Around 12.30 she begins to prepare lunch. She gets out the fish and the vegetables from the fridge.
Half an hour later she puts the fish in the oven and cooks the vegetables.
At 2.00 on the dot she carries the lunch to the dining room.
After lunch she makes a cup of coffee for her husband.
At around 3.30 she stacks the dirty plates in the dishwasher.

Answers:

1.	*A las 10 pone la lavadora.*	At 10.00 she puts on the washing-machine.
2.	*Empieza a preparar la comida sobre las 12.30.*	She begins to prepare lunch at around 12.30.
3.	*Friega el suelo a las 10.05.*	She washes the floor at 10.05.
4.	*Saca el pescado de la nevera.*	She gets the fish from the fridge.
5.	*No, la familia come en la mesa del comedor.*	No, the Trujillo family eat lunch in the dining room.
6.	*Prepara un café para su marido.*	She makes a cup of coffee for her husband.
7.	*Pone los platos sucios en el lavaplatos.*	She puts the dirty plates in the dishwasher.
8.	*Sobre las 3.30.*	At around 3.30.

Exercise 4.34
Pupil's Book: Page 104; Audio CD 2 track: 20

In this exercise, which is quite difficult, pupils listen to the conversation between Paco and his family over lunch. The track may have to be played a number of times for pupils to be in a position to answer the questions that follow, particularly question 10. For those using the CD Rom, clicking on the ? icon reveals the answers.

Audio CD 2 Track 20:

Mamá:	*¡Venga, niños! A la mesa. La comida ya está puesta. Ya son las dos.*
Paco:	*¿Qué hay de primer plato?*
Mamá:	*Pues hoy tenemos una buena sopa de fideos .....*
Paco:	*Pero mamá ..... ¡siempre comemos lo mismo!*
Mamá:	*¡Anda, come y calla!*
Laura:	*Mamá, pásame el agua, por favor.*
Mamá:	*Toma.*
Laura:	*Está riquísima la sopa, mamá.*
Mamá:	*¡Menos mal!*
Padre:	*¿Qué tal el colegio, chicos?*
Paco:	*Estupendo, papá……. ¿Qué hay de segundo, mamá?*
Mamá:	*Pescado, o sea tu plato preferido – lubina a la sal con verduras.*
Paco:	*Ummm, ¡Qué rico! ¡Para chuparse los dedos…..!*
Laura:	*¿Y de postre?*
Mamá:	*Flan con nata.*
Padre:	*¡Ay, ya son las tres y tengo que volver a la oficina….!*

Translation:

Mamá:	Come on, children. To the table. Lunch is ready. It is already 2.00.
Paco:	What is for first course?
Mamá:	Well, today we are having a nice noodle soup and afterwards...
Paco:	But mum, we always have the same for lunch!
Mamá:	Come on, eat and be quiet!
Laura:	Mum, pass the water, please.
Mamá:	Here it is.
Laura:	The soup is delicious, mum.
Mamá:	Not bad!
Padre:	How's school, children?
Paco:	Brilliant, Dad. What is for the main course, mum?
Mamá:	Fish, that is to say your favourite dish – sea bass cooked in salt with vegetables.
Paco:	Ummm, How delicious! Absolutely scrumptious!
Laura:	And for pudding?
Mamá:	Creme caramel with cream.
Padre:	Ah, it's 3.00 already and I have to get back to the office!

Answers:

1. *Son las dos.* — It is two o'clock.
2. *Hay una buena sopa de fideos.* — It is a nice noodle soup.
3. *Paco no está contento.* — Paco is not satisfied.
4. *Paco no está contento porque siempre come lo mismo!* — Paco is not satisfied because he always eats the same.
5. *Está riquísima la sopa.* — The soup is delicious.
6. *Paco piensa que es estupendo.* — Paco thinks that it is brilliant.
7. *El segundo plato es lubina a la sal con verduras.* — The main course is sea bass cooked in salt with vegetables.
8. *De postre hay flan con nata.* — For pudding there is creme caramel with cream.
9. *El padre vuelve a la oficina a las tres.* — The father returns to his office at 3.00.
10. *A Paco le gusta mucho la lubina.* — The boy really likes the sea bass.

Exercise 4.35
Pupil's Book: Page 105.

In this exercise, four pictures of Paco in the bathroom are displayed. Pupils have to write a sentence using a reflexive verb to describe what he is doing and when.

Suggested answers:

1. *Paco se levanta y se baña a las 7.00.*
2. *A las 7.10 se afeita en el cuarto de baño.*
3. *A las 7.20 se limpia los dientes.*
4. *A las 7.30 se peina.*

Those using the CD Rom can see and hear the suggested answers by clicking on the **?** icons.

Exercise 4.36
Pupil's Book: Page 106.

This exercise allows pupils to practise their written work while describing their homes and the way these are furnished.

Exercise 4.37
Pupil's Book: Page 106.

This exercise allows pupils to practise talking about the various rooms of the house and how these are furnished. Those using the CD Rom can see the the questions displayed and, by clicking on each one, hear the questions being posed, and by clicking on the Union Flag icon, see them translated.

¿Qué haces en?

¿Qué haces en la sala de estar?	What do you do in the dining room?
¿Qué haces en la cocina?	What do you do in the kitchen?
¿Qué haces en tu dormitorio?	What do you do in your bedroom?
¿Qué haces en el comedor?	What do you do in the dining room?
¿Qué haces en el cuarto de baño?	What do you do in the bathroom.

¿A qué hora?

¿A qué hora te levantas?	What time do you get up?
¿A qué hora te acuestas?	What time do you go to bed?

¿Dónde?

¿Dónde ves la televisión?	Where do you watch television?
¿Dónde te lavas?	Where do you wash?
¿Dónde desayunas?	Where do you have breakfast?
¿Dónde comes?	Where do you have lunch?
¿Dónde escuchas música?	Where do you listen to music?
¿Dónde haces los deberes?	Where do you do your homework?
¿Dónde duermes?	Where do you go to sleep?

¿Qué muebles hay en?

¿Qué muebles hay en la sala de estar?	Which furniture is in the sitting-room?
¿Qué muebles hay en el comedor?	Which furniture is in the dining room
¿Qué muebles hay en la cocina?	Which furniture is in the kitchen?

¿Dónde está?

¿Dónde está el dormitorio de tus padres?	Where is your parents' bedroom?
¿Dónde está tu dormitorio?	Where is your bedroom?
¿Dónde está el cuarto de baño?	Where is the bathroom?
¿Dónde está la televisión?	Where is the television?
¿Dónde está el sofá?	Where is the sofa?
¿Dónde está el teléfono?	Where is the telephone?

UNIT 5: En el pueblo

About the unit

In this unit pupils learn about places in town and to ask for and give simple directions. They learn to talk about the weather and names of countries.

Where the unit fits in

This unit extends knowledge and learning about verbs to using the positive imperative of regular *-ar*, *-er* and *-ir* verbs.

It extends the use of prepositions.

It prepares for unit 6 '*Pasatiempos*' by defining where activities take place and sets out all persons of the irregular verb *ir*.

New language content:

- the irregular verb *ir*
- positive imperative form of regular verbs, second and third persons singular

New contexts:

- places in town
- points of the compass and maps
- following and giving directions
- seasons
- weather

This unit is expected to take 12–15 hours.

Expectations

At the end of this unit most pupils will: name common places in town on a map; say where one place is situated in relation to another using common prepositions; ask their way to common places in a town and understand the reply; respond to a request for directions with the correct information; understand how regular imperatives are formed in the second and third persons singular and use them correctly and appropriately; understand simple expressions to describe the weather and enquire what the weather is like in given places; have some knowledge of countries where Spanish is the main language spoken.

Some pupils will not have made so much progress and will: ask the way to a number of key locations in a town; understand and give simple directions; place or draw symbols on a map to indicate weather conditions; have a limited knowledge of Spanish-speaking countries.

Some pupils will have progressed further and will: understand and give more complex directions to a specified place; describe more accurately where one place is situated in relation to another; repeat instructions in the first person singular to indicate comprehension; interpret a map to work out directions; make inferences about weather conditions from pictures; find out basic geographical information about selected Spanish-speaking countries.

El pueblo
Pupil's Book: Page 110.

Those using the CD Rom can display the map of the town from the pupil's book. Clicking on an item reveals the caption for that item.

Exercise 5.1
Pupil's Book: Page 111; Audio CD 2 tracks: 21-24

This exercise allows pupils to practise listening to people asking for and giving the directions.

Audio CD 2 track 21:

Señor 1:   *¿Dónde está la farmacia, por favor?*
Señorita: *Está muy cerca, al lado del supermercado.*
Señor 1:   *Gracias.*
Señorita: *De nada, Adiós.*

Translation:

Señor 1:   Where is the chemist, please?
Señorita: It is very near, next to the supermarket.
Señor 1:   Thank you.
Señorita: Not at all, goodbye.

Audio CD 2 track 22:

Señora 1:   *¡Hola, buenos días! ¿Me puede decir dónde está el teatro, por favor?*
Señorita: *Sí, está al lado de la plaza de toros.*
Señora 1:   *Pero ¿dónde está la plaza de toros?*
Señorita: *Está enfrente del ayuntamiento.*

Translation:

Señora 1:   Hello, good morning! Can you tell me where the theatre is, please?
Señorita: Yes, it is next to the bull ring.
Señora 1:   But where is the bull ring?
Señorita: It is opposite the town hall.

Audio CD 2 track 23:

Chico 1:   *Buenas tardes Señorita, ¿dónde está la iglesia, por favor?*
Señorita: *La iglesia está al lado del estadio.*
Chico 1:   *Ah sí, gracias, adiós.*
Señorita: *De nada, adiós.*

Translation:

Chico 1:   Good afternoon miss, where is the church please?
Señorita: The church is next to the stadium.
Chico 1:   Oh yes, thank you, goodbye.
Señorita: Not at all, goodbye.

Audio CD 2 track 24:

Chica 1:   *Hola ¿dónde está el supermercado?*
Señorita: *¿El supermercado? Sí, está muy, muy cerca, enfrente del hotel 'Sol'.*
Chica 1:   *Muy bien. Gracias.*
Señorita: *De nada, ¡que lo pase bien! Adiós.*
Chica 1:   *Adiós.*

Translation:

Chica 1:   Hello, where is the supermarket?
Señorita: The supermarket? Yes, it is very, very near, opposite the Hotel Sol.
Chica 1:   Very good, thank you.
Señorita: Not at all. Have a good day! Goodbye.
Chica 1:   Goodbye.

Answers:

1.   *La farmacia está al lado del supermercado.*
2.   *El teatro está al lado de la plaza de toros. La plaza de toros está enfrente del ayuntamiento.*
3.   *La iglesia está al lado del estadio.*
4.   *El supermercado está enfrente del hotel 'Sol'.*

Those using the CD Rom can play the four audio tracks and display the answers on the screen by clicking on the **?** icons.

Exercise 5.2
Pupil's Book: Page 111.

1.   *El teatro está bastante lejos. Está cerca de la plaza de toros.*
2.   *La discoteca está detrás de la iglesia.*
3.   *La panadería está enfrente del mercado.*
4.   *La catedral está a las afueras del pueblo.*
5.   *La plaza de toros está cerca del bar.*
6.   *La iglesia está enfrente del ayuntamiento.*
7.   *El estadio está cerca del supermercado.*
8.   *La farmacia está muy cerca del banco.*

Those using the CD Rom can display the answers on the screen by clicking on the Spanish flag icons.

Exercise 5.3
Pupil's Book: Page 111.

This exercise allows pupils to look at the map on page 110 of the pupil's book and to ask each other where the listed places are. Those using the CD Rom can click on each place to play a suggested answer, as shown below.

Suggested answers:

1.   *La plaza está en el centro del pueblo.*
2.   *El mercado está en la plaza..*
3.   *El hotel está enfrente del supermercado.*
4.   *El teatro está detrás de la panadería.*

5.   La panadería está delante del teatro.
6.   La piscina está detrás de la plaza de toros.
7.   La plaza de toros está al lado del teatro.
8.   El banco está enfrente del cine.

Ir = to go
Pupil's Book: Page 112.

Teachers may wish to compare this irregular verb with the French verb *aller*.

	SPANISH		FRENCH	
	Singular	**Plural**	**Singular**	**Plural**
1st person	Voy	Vamos	vais	allons
2nd person	Vas	Vais	vais	allez
3rd person	Va	Van	va	vont

Those using the CD Rom can click on each verb for to hear it pronounced.

¿Adónde vas?
Pupil's Book: Page 112.

For those using the CD Rom, clicking on each phrase allows pupils to hear that phrase pronounced.

Hoy yo voy al bar.	Today I am going to the bar.
Tú vas al teatro, ¿verdad?	You are going to the theatre, aren't you?.
Mi madre va a la farmacia a comprar aspirinas	My mother is going to the chemist to buy aspirins.
Los sábados vamos a la discoteca.	On Saturdays we go to the disco.
Vosotros vais al restaurante francés.	You are going to the French restaurant.
Los domingos mis padres van a la iglesia	On Sundays my parents go to church.

Exercise 5.4
Pupil's Book: Page 113.
Answers:

1.   *Voy a la plaza de toros.*
2.   *Vas a la estación.*
3.   *Mi familia va a la iglesia los domingos.*
4.   *No vamos al colegio los sábados.*
5.   *¿Usted va al cine por las tardes?*
6.   *¿Vais al pueblo?*
7.   *Mis hermanas siempre van a las tiendas.*
8.   *Ustedes van al supermercado.*

Those using the CD Rom can display the answers on the screen by clicking on the Spanish flag icons.

Exercise 5. 5
Pupil's Book: Page 113; Audio CD 2 tracks: 25-29

In this exercise, pupils hear five characters saying where they are going that day. Pupils have to fill in the table by saying where each character is going and where that place is. Those using the CD Rom can display the answers on the screen by clicking on the **?** icons.

Audio CD 2 Track 25:

1.

Carolina:	Hola, Alfredo. ¿Qué tal?	Hello, Alfredo. How are you?
Alfredo:	Muy bien.	Very well.
Carolina:	¿Adónde vas esta tarde?	Where are you going this afternoon?
Alfredo:	Voy a la cafetería Lemán con mis amigos.	I am going to the cafe Lemán with my friends.
Carolina:	¿Dónde está exactamente?	Where is it exactly?
Alfredo:	Está cerca de mi casa, en la Calle Mayor.	It is near my house, in the Calle Mayor.

Audio CD 2 Track 26:

2.

Carolina:	Hola, Isabel. ¿Cómo estás?	Hello, Isabel. How are you?
Isabel:	Yo, estupendamente.	Me? Brilliant.
Carolina:	¿Adónde vas hoy después del colegio?	Where are you going today after school?
Isabel:	Voy a la piscina.	I am going to the swimming pool.
Carolina:	¿Dónde está la piscina?	Where is the swimming pool?
Isabel:	Está detrás del Hotel Las Vegas.	It is behind the Hotel Las Vegas.

Audio CD 2 Track 27:

3.

Juan:	Hola Rafael. ¿Qué hay?	Hello Rafael. What are you up to?
Rafael:	Pues, nada en particular.	Well, nothing in particular.
Juan:	¿Adónde vas hoy?	Where are you going today?
Rafael:	Pues esta tarde voy al cine.	Well, this afternoon I am going to the cimema.
Juan:	¿Dónde está el cine?	Where is the cinema?
Rafael:	Está enfrente de la estación.	It is opposite the station.

Audio CD 2 Track 28:

4.

Rafael:	Hola Mari Carmen. ¿Qué tal?	Hello Mari Carmen. How are you doing?
Mari Carmen:	Pues, bien gracias.	Um, well thanks.
Rafael:	¿Adónde vas normalmente los domingos?	Where do you normally go on Sundays?
Mari Carmen:	Por la mañana voy a la iglesia con mi familia.	In the morning I go to church with my family.
Rafael:	¿Dónde está la iglesia?	Where is the church?
Mari Carmen:	Está bastante lejos de mi casa, en la Calle Valencia.	It is quite a long way from my house, in the Calle Valencia.

Audio CD 2 Track 29:

5.

Rafael:	*¿Y tú? Raquel, ¿Cómo estás?*	And you, Raquel. How are you?
Raquel:	*Pues...fatal.*	Well...awful.
Rafael:	*¿Adónde vas ahora?*	Where are you going now?
Raquel:	*Pues voy a la farmacia a comprar aspirinas.*	Well I am going to the chemist to buy some asprins.
Rafael:	*¿Dónde está la farmacia?*	Where is the chemist?
Raquel:	*Está al lado del Banco de España.*	It is next to the Banco de España.

Answers:

Alfredo	*va a la cafetería.*	*Está en la Calle Mayor.*
Isabel	*va a la piscina.*	*Está detrás del Hotel Las Vegas.*
Rafael	*va al cine.*	*Está enfrente de la estación.*
Mari Carmen	*va a la iglesia.*	*Está en la Calle Valencia.*
Raquel	*va a la farmacia.*	*Está al lado del Banco de España.*

¿Por dónde se va a?
Pupil's Book: Page 113.

Those using the CD Rom can illustrate the use of *¿por dónde se va a?*, and the appropriate responses using *hay que* and *tiene que*, by accessing four short practice dialogues as follows:

1.

Señora 1:	*¿Por dónde se va a la farmacia?*	How do you get to the chemist?
Señorita:	*Hay que subir esta calle.*	You have to go up this street.

2.

Señor:	*¿Por dónde se va a la catedral?*	How do you get to the cathedral?
Señorita:	*Tiene que cruzar la plaza.*	You have to cross the square.

3.

Señora 2:	*¿Por dónde se va al ayuntamiento?*	How do you get to the town-hall?
Señorita:	*Hay que tomar la primera calle a l a derecha.*	You have to take the first street on the right.

4.

Juan:	*¿Por dónde se va a la discoteca, amigo?*	How do you get to the disco, friend?
Eduardo:	*Tienes que bajar esta calle y tomar la segunda a la izquierda.*	You have to go down this street and take the second on the left.

Exercise 5.6
Pupil's Book: Page 114.

1.   How do you get to the bakery?
    You have to continue straight ahead and take the 2nd on the left.

2.   How do you get to the Banco de España?
    You have to turn to the right, and the bank is opposite the Aurrerá supermarket.

3.   How do you get to the Cervantes Theatre?
    You have to go down this street and then take the first on the left. It is 100 metres away.

4.   How do you get to the Municipal Market?
    You have to carry along as far as the station. It is opposite.

Those using the CD Rom can listen to the Spanish sentences and then display the translations by clicking on the Union Flag icons.

Exercise 5.7
Pupil's Book: Page 114.

This exercise allows pupils to practise giving and receiving directions. Those using the CD Rom can display the map on the screen. Clicking on various parts of the map puts a question mark over one of the key sites, and pupils then have to ask how to get to that place.

Imperatives
Pupil's Book: Page 115.

Pupils learnt some commonly used familiar imperatives in Unit 1. They now learn how to form the polite form imperatives, before moving on to the formation of familiar form ones on page 117. Those using the CD Rom can display the information on the screen and hear each word pronounced by clicking on it.

Exercise 5.8
Pupil's Book: Page 115; Audio tracks: 30-34

In this exercise, pupils hear five characters asking for and receiving directions. Pupils have to write down where each person wanted to go and how they get there. Those using the CD Rom can display this information on the screen by clicking on the **?** icons.

Audio CD 2 Track 30:

Número 1.

Carolina:	*Perdone, señor, ¿Por dónde se va al Ayuntamiento, por favor?*
Miguel:	*Siga todo recto y está a 100 metros, a la derecha.*
Carolina:	*Gracias.*
Miguel:	*De nada. Adiós.*
Carolina:	*Adiós.*

Translation:

Carolina:	Excuse me, sir. How do you get to the Town-hall, please?
Miguel:	Continue straight and it is 100 metres on the right.
Carolina:	Thanks.
Miguel:	Not at all. Goodbye.
Carolina:	Goodbye.

Audio CD 2 Track 31:

Número 2.

Elena:	*Perdone, señora. ¿Por dónde se va al Hotel las Vegas?*
Señora:	*Cruce la plaza y está enfrente.*
Elena:	*Muchas gracias.*
Señora:	*De nada. Adiós.*

Translation:

Elena:	Excuse me, madam. How do you get to the Hotel Las Vegas?
Señora:	Cross the square and it is opposite.
Elena:	Many thanks.
Señora:	Not at all. Goodbye.

Audio CD 2 Track 32:

Número 3.

Miguel:	*Oiga, señorita, ¿Por dónde se va al estadio Bernabeu, por favor?*
Elena:	*Pues …Tome la primera calle a la izquierda y está al final de la calle.*
Miguel:	*Vale. Gracias*
Elena:	*De nada. Adiós.*

Translation:

Miguel:	Hey, miss. How do you get to the Bernabeu stadium, please?
Elena:	Well...Take the first street on the left and it is at the end of the street.
Miguel:	Okay. Thanks.
Elena:	Not at all. Goodbye.

Audio CD 2 Track 33:

Número 4.

Vanessa:	*Por favor, señora, ¿Por dónde se va a la estación?*
Señora:	*¡Uf, está bastante lejos! Suba esta calle, luego doble a la derecha en el semáforo. La estación está a unos 200 metros a la izquierda.*
Vanessa:	*Gracias. Adiós.*
Señora:	*De nada.*

Translation:

Vanessa:	Please, madam. How do you get to the station?
Señora:	Ugh, it's quite a long way away! Carry on along this street, then turn right at the traffic lights. The station is about 200 metres on the left.
Vanessa:	Thank you. Goodbye.
Señora:	Not at all.

Audio CD 2 Track 34:

Número 5.

Alfredo:	*Perdone señorita. ¿Cómo se va a Correos?*
Vanessa:	*Pues, está muy cerca de aquí. Cruce la calle y está justo enfrente. ¡Mírelo!*
Alfredo:	*Vale. Muchas gracias.*
Vanessa:	*De nada. ¡Hasta luego!*
Alfredo:	*Adiós.*

Translation:

Alfredo:	Excuse me, miss. How do you get to the Post Office?
Vanessa:	Well, it is very near here. Cross the street and it is there straight in front of you. Look!
Alfredo:	Okay. Thank you very much.
Vanessa:	Not at all. See you!
Alfredo:	Goodbye.

Answers to questions:

1.　　(a)　*Quiere ir al ayuntamiento.*
　　　(b)　*Tiene que seguir todo recto y está a 100 metros, a la derecha.*

2.　　(a)　*Quiere ir al Hotel las Vegas.*
　　　(b)　*Tiene que cruzar la plaza y está enfrente.*

3.　　(a)　*Quiere ir al estadio Bernabeu.*
　　　(b)　*Tiene que tomar la primera calle a la izquierda y está al final de la calle.*

4.　　(a)　*Quiere ir a la estación.*
　　　(b)　*Tiene que subir esta calle, luego doblar a la derecha en el semáforo. La estación está a unos 200 metros a la izquierda.*

5.　　(a)　*Quiere ir a Correos.*
　　　(b)　*Tiene que cruzar la calle y está justo enfrente.*

Exercise 5.9
Pupil's Book: Page 115.

1.　　How do you get to the castle, please?
　　　Take the first street on the left.

2.　　How do you get to the main square, please?
　　　Take the second street on the right.

3.　　How do you get to the RENFE station, please?
　　　Take the third street on the left.

4.　　How do you get to the tourist office, please?
　　　Cross the square and it is on the left.

Those using the CD Rom can hear the sentences and display the translations by clicking on the Union Flag icons.

Exercise 5.10
Pupil's Book: Page 116.

The translations are displayed by clicking on the ? icon.

1.　　*Baje la calle.*
2.　　*Cruce la plaza.*
3.　　*Siga todo recto.*
4.　　*Tome la primera calle a la derecha.*
5.　　*Tome la segunda calle a la izquierda.*
6.　　*Doble a la derecha en el semáforo.*
7.　　*Suba esta calle.*
8.　　*Está allí, al lado de la iglesia.*

Those using the CD Rom can hear the sentences and display the translations by clicking on the Spanish flag icons.

Exercise 5.11
Pupil's Book: Page 116.

This exercise practises asking for and giving directions to various places in the town. For those using the CD, a series of questions is randomly generated and displayed and pupils have to practise answering them.

Random questions:

¿Por dónde se va al ayuntamiento?
¿Por dónde se va al banco?
¿Por dónde se va al bar?
¿Por dónde se va a Correos?
¿Por dónde se va al cine?
¿Por dónde se va al estadio?
¿Por dónde se va al hotel?
¿Por dónde se va al mercado?
¿Por dónde se va al pueblo?
¿Por dónde se va al restaurante?
¿Por dónde se va al supermercado?
¿Por dónde se va al teatro?
¿Por dónde se va a la biblioteca?
¿Por dónde se va a la cafetería?
¿Por dónde se va a la catedral?
¿Por dónde se va a la discoteca?
¿Por dónde se va a la farmacia?
¿Por dónde se va a la iglesia?
¿Por dónde se va a la panadería?
¿Por dónde se va a la piscina?
¿Por dónde se va a la plaza?
¿Por dónde se va a la plaza de toros?
¿Por dónde se va a la tienda?

Exercise 5.12
Pupil's Book: Page 116; Audio CD 2 track: 35

In this exercise, pupils read and/or listen to the passage and then answer true or false to the questions that follow. Teachers may choose to do this as a listening exercise only, or they may wish their pupils to follow the dialogue in the book.

Audio CD 2 track 35:

El Peatón:	*"Perdone, señor, ¿para ir a la catedral, por favor?"*
Señor:	*"Lo siento, no soy de aquí".*
El Peatón:	*"Oiga, señorita. ¿Por dónde se va a la catedral, por favor?"*
Señorita:	*"¿Va Usted en coche o andando?"*
El Peatón:	*"Andando".*
Señorita:	*"¡Uf, está un poco lejos!"*
El Peatón:	*"Hable un poco más despacio, por favor. Soy extranjero.*

Señorita:	"Ay, lo siento….. Pues tiene que seguir todo recto, ¿comprende?, hasta el final de esta calle. Usted verá la biblioteca municipal en la esquina. Pues, coja la calle a la derecha , que se llama Calle Princesa, y baje esa calle hasta el primer semáforo. Allí hay que cruzar la plaza y la catedral está justo enfrente. ¿Vale?"
El Peatón:	"Un momento,…. todo recto hasta el final, luego a la derecha hasta el semáforo y allí tengo que cruzar la plaza, ¿no?"
Señorita:	"Eso es, señor."
El Peatón:	"Muchas gracias, señorita."

Translation:

El Peatón:	Excuse me, sir. (How does one) get to the cathedral, please?
Señor:	I'm sorry, I am not from here.
El Peatón:	Hay, miss. How do you get to the cathedral, please?
Señorita:	Are you in a car or on foot?
El Peatón:	On foot.
Señorita:	Urr, it is quite far!
El Peatón:	Speak a little slower, please. I am a foreigner.
Señorita:	Oh, sorry...Well, you have to continue straight, understand?, to the end of this street. You will see the public library on the corner. Then, take the street on the right, which is called Calle Princesa, and go down that street to the first set of lights. There you have to cross the square and the cathedral is right opposite. Okay?
El Peatón:	One moment....straight on to the end, then to the right up to the lights, and there I have to cross the square, yes?
Señorita:	That's right, sir.
El Peatón:	Thank you very much.

Answers:

1.	El peatón va a la iglesia.	False (he is going to the **cathedral**).
2.	El señor es de allí.	False (he is **not** from there).
3.	El peatón va en coche.	False (he is going on **foot**).
4.	La señorita habla muy despacio.	False (he has to ask her to speak more slowly).
5.	La catedral está lejos.	True.
6.	El peatón tiene que cruzar la calle.	False (he has to cross the **square**).
7.	Hay una piscina en la esquina.	False (there is a **public library** on the corner).
8.	La calle a la derecha se llama "Calle Princesa".	True.
9.	El peatón tiene que subir la Calle Princesa.	False (he has to go **down** Calle Princesa).
10.	La catedral está enfrente de la plaza.	True.

Imperatives: familiar form
Pupil's Book: Page 117.

Pupils have already met some familiar forms of the imperative, but now learn how to form them themselves. Those using the CD Rom can click on the words to hear them pronounced.

Exercise 5.13
Pupil's Book: Page 118; Audio CD 2 track: 36

This exercise allows pupils to hear a conversation between Esteban and Paloma. For those using the CD Rom, the six sentences are displayed (with gaps) and pupils drag and drop the answers (shown in bold) onto the gaps.

Audio CD 2 track 36:

Esteban: *Oye, ¿por qué no vamos a la nueva discoteca el sábado?*

Paloma: *Pues, sí. Es una buena idea. ¿Pero cómo se va?*

Esteban: *Desde tu casa coge el autobús número 3 que para en el Corte Inglés, ¿vale? Luego baja por la Calle Mayor y cuando llegues al primer semáforo toma la primera a la derecha. Sube esa calle hasta el final y luego toma la segunda a la izquierda, y la discoteca está a unos doscientos metros al lado de un supermercado.*

Paloma: *Entonces, cojo el autobús número 3 hasta el Corte Inglés, ¿no? Luego bajo por la Calle Mayor hasta el primer semáforo. Es eso, ¿no? Cojo la primera a la derecha. Subo hasta el final y luego tomo la segunda a la izquierda y la discoteca está al lado de un supermercado.*

Esteban: *¡Perfecto! Entonces nos vemos allí el sábado a las 10, ¿vale?*

Paloma: *¡Estupendo! Hasta el sábado, pues.*

Translation:

Esteban: Hay, why don't we go to the new disco on Saturday?

Paloma: Well, yes. It's a good idea. But how do we get there?

Esteban: From your house take the number 3 bus which stops in the Corte Inglés, okay? Then go down the Calle Mayor and when you get to the first set of lights, take the first on the right. Go up that street to the end and then take the second on the left, and the disco is about 200 metres away, next to a supermarket.

Paloma: So, I take the number 3 bus to the Corte Inglés, yes? Then I go down the Calle Mayor to the first set of lights. That's right, yes? I take the first on the right. I go up to the end and then I take the second on the left and the disco is next to a supermarket.

Esteban: Perfect! Then, see you there on Saturday at 10.00, okay?

Paloma: Superb! Until Saturday, then.

Answers:

1.   *Hay que coger el autobús número **3**...*
2.   *...hasta el **Corte Inglés**.*
3.   *Entonces hay que bajar por la **Calle Mayor**...*
4.   *...y cuando llegues al **primer** semáforo,*
5.   *hay que tomar la **primera** a la derecha.*
6.   *Entonces, hay que subir esa calle hasta **el final**...*
7.   *...y luego tomar la segunda a la **izquierda**.*
8.   *La discoteca está a **200** metros...*
9.   *...al lado de un **supermercado**.*
10.   *Hay que estar allí el sábado a las **10**.*

Exercise 5.14
Pupil's Book: Page 118.

This exercise allows pupils to practise writing directions to their homes from a landmark such as the nearest station.

Exercise 5.15
Pupil's Book: Page 118.

This exercise is similar to the previous one but is a speaking exercise. Pupils may find it useful to refer to their written answers to Exercise 5.14 when practising this with their partners.

Vocabulario 5.1
Pupil's Book: Page 118.

The vocabulary from the pupil's book should now be copied down, learnt and tested. Those using the CD Rom can display it on the screen.

Los países del mundo
Pupil's Book: Page 119.

This is a good time to remind pupils of where Spanish is spoken (see Unit 2, page 49). Those using the CD Rom can display the map of the Americas on one screen and that of Europe on another.

Exercise 5.16
Pupil's Book: Page 120; Audio CD 2 tracks: 37-38.

In this exercise pupils practise asking each other where they come from and which language they speak. They should first study and listen to the examples, first the familiar form one (track 37) and then the polite form one (track 38).

Audio CD 2 Track 37:

"¿De dónde eres?"	Where are you from?
"Soy de Argentina."	I am from Argentina.
"¿De qué nacionalidad eres?"	What nationality are you?
"Soy argentina y vivo en Buenos Aires."	I am Argentinian and I live in Buenos Aires.
"¿Qué idioma hablas?"	Which language do you speak?
"Hablo español."	I speak Spanish.

Audio CD 2 Track 38:

¿De dónde es Usted?	Where are you from?
Soy de Méjico.	I am from Mexico.
¿De qué nacionalidad es Vd?	What nationality are you?
Soy mexicana y vivo en Guadalajara.	I am Mexican and I live in Guadalajara.
¿Qué idioma habla?	Which language do you speak?
Hablo español.	I speak Spanish.

Those using the CD Rom can watch the two examples as simple animations. They can then display a list of countries in Central America, South America and Europe with the appropriate nationality, capital city and language spoken, as follows:

País	Nacionalidad	Ciudad	Idioma
Centroamérica			
Méjico	mejicano	Ciudad de México	español
Guatemala	guatemalteco	Ciudad de Guatemala	español
Nicaragua	nicaragüense	Managua	español
El Salvador	salvadoreño	San Salvador	español
Honduras	hondureño	Tegucigalpa	español
Costa Rica	costarriqueño	San José	español
Panamá	panameño	Panamá	español
Sudamérica			
Venezuela	venezolano	Caracas	español
Colombia	colombiano	Bogotá	español
Perú	peruano	Lima	español
Bolivia	boliviano	La Paz	español
Ecuador	ecuatoriano	Quito	español
Paraguay	paraguayo	Asunción	español
Uruguay	uruguayo	Montevideo	español
Chile	chileno	Santiago	español
Argentina	argentino	Buenos Aires	español
Europa			
Inglaterra	inglés	Londres	inglés
Irlanda	irlandés	Dublín	inglés
Escocia	escocés	Edimburgo	inglés
Gales	galés	Cardiff	inglés
Francia	francés	París	francés
España	español	Madrid	español
Portugal	portugués	Lisboa	portugués
Italia	italiano	Roma	italiano
Alemania	alemán	Berlín	alemán
Bélgica	belga	Bruselas	belga
Holanda	holandés	Amsterdam	holandés
Grecia	griego	Atenas	griego
Dinamarca	danés	Copenhague	danés
Noruega	noruego	Oslo	noruego
Suecia	sueco	Estocolmo	sueco
Finlandia	finlandés	Helsinki	finlandés

Exercise 5.17
Pupil's Book: Page 120; Audio CD 2 tracks: 39-44

In this exercise, pupils read and/or listen to the descriptions and have to guess which country is being described.

Audio CD 2 Track 39:

1. *Está al sur de Rusia. Es un país muy grande pero no se habla ni inglés ni español.*
   It is to the south of Russia. It is a very big country but neither English nor Spanish is spoken.

Audio CD 2 Track 40:

2. *Está en el norte de Sudamérica al lado de Colombia. La capital es Caracas. Se habla español.*
    It is in the north of South America next to Colombia. The capital is Caracas. Spanish is spoken.

Audio CD 2 Track 41:

3. *Es un país pequeño de Centroamérica entre Panamá y Nicaragua. También se habla español.*
    It is a little country in Central America between Panama and Nicaragua. Spanish is spoken here also.

Audio CD 2 Track 42:

4. *Es un país bastante grande en el sur de Europa donde se habla español.*
    It is quite a big country in the south of Europe where Spanish is spoken.

Audio CD 2 Track 43:

5. *Está en el norte de Europa. Es una isla pequeña donde se habla inglés.*
    It is in the north of Europe. It is a little island where English is spoken.

Audio CD 2 Track 44:

6. *Es un país en el este de Norteamérica donde se habla inglés y también francés.*
    It is a country in the east of North America where English is spoken and also French.

Answers

1. *China*
2. *Venezuela*
3. *Costa Rica*
4. *España*
5. *Inglaterra*
6. *Canadá*

Those using the CD Rom can display the answers by clicking on the ? icons.

Exercise 5.18
Pupil's Book: Page 121; Audio CD 2 tracks: 45-50

In this exercise pupils listen to the six characters. They then copy and fill in the table with (1) country of origin; and (2) where they live.

Audio CD 2 track 45:

1. *¡Hola! Me llamo Laura. Soy de Costa Rica. Vivo en la capital San José con mi familia. No es una ciudad muy grande pero me gusta.*
    Hello. My name is Laura. I am from Costa Rica. I live in the capital, San José, with my family. It is not a very big city but I like it.

Audio CD 2 track 46:

2. *¡Hola! Mi nombre es Brita. Soy de Estocolmo, en Suecia, pero ahora vivo en España. Prefiero España porque hace mucho sol.*
    Hello. My name is Brita. I am from Stockholm, in Sweeden, but now I live in Spain. I prefer Spain because there is lots of sun.

Audio CD 2 track 47:

3.   *¡Hola! Yo soy Damián. Soy de Escocia. Mi padre es colombiano pero yo soy escocés como mi madre. Vivimos en Glasgow.*

Hello. I am Damián. I am from Scotland. My father is Colombian but I am Scottish, like my mother. We live in Glasgow.

Audio CD 2 track 48:

4.   *¡Hola! Yo me llamo Jacqueline. Soy francesa, de Estrasburgo, pero vivo en Barcelona desde hace muchos años. Me gusta mucho vivir aquí porque es una ciudad muy interesante.*

Hello. My name is Jacqueline. I am French, from Strasbourg, but I have lived in Barcelona for many years. I really like living here because it is a very interesting city.

Audio CD 2 track 49:

5.   *¡Hola! Soy José. Nací en un pequeño pueblo en el sur de España pero ahora vivimos en Málaga. Hay unas playas muy bonitas. Me gusta vivir aquí.*

Hello. I am José. I was born in a little town in the south of Spain but we now live in Málaga. There are some very beautiful beaches. I like living here.

Audio CD 2 track 50:

6.   *¡Hola! Soy Dora. Vivo en Nueva York, en los Estados Unidos, con mis padres y mis dos hermanos, pero nací en Perú. Tengo nacionalidad peruana y hablo español e inglés.*

Hello. I am Dora. I live in New York, in the United States, with my parents and my two brothers, but I was born in Peru. I have Peruvian nationality and I speak Spanish and English.

Answers:

1.	Laura	Costa Rica	San José
2.	Brita	Estocolmo	España
3.	Damián	Escocia	Glasgow
4.	Jacqueline	Francia	Barcelona
5.	José	España	Málaga
6.	Dora	Perú	Nueva York

Those using the CD Rom can display the answers by clicking on the **?** icons.

Exercise 5.19
Pupil's Book: Page 121.

This exercise allows pupils practice at quite a complicated reading passage on which they have to answer questions. Those using the CD Rom can play the audio track of this passage and display the answers to the questions by clicking on the **?** icons.

Translation:

Mexico is a country situated in the extreme south of North America. It is bordered to the north by the United States; to the east by the Gulf of Mexico and the Caribbean Sea; to the south by Belize and Guatemala and to the west by the Pacific Ocean.

Mexico is the Hispanic country with the greatest number of inhabitants and its capital, Mexico City, is the largest city on the planet – it has more than 20 million uinhabitants.

The economy has two main sectors: agriculture and mining. Mexico has a very varied agriculture, from cereals to tropical crops such as sugar cane, coffee, cocoa, cotton etc. It is the world's 6th (largest) producer of petroleum and the 8th (largest) for natural gas.

The official language of the country is Spanish and its currency is the Mexican peso. If one day you go to Mexico you must visit the incredible museum of Anthropology and History in the capital and, on the outskirts, the famous Pyramids of Teotihuacán.

Answers:

1.   *Méjico está situado en el extremo meridional de América del norte.*
2.   *Los Estados Unidos están al norte de Méjico.*
3.   *El mar al este de Méjico se llama el mar Caribe.*
4.   *El océano Pacífico está al oeste de Méjico.*
5.   *Hay más de veinte millones de habitantes en la capital.*
6.   *Las dos sectores principales son la actividad agraria y la minera.*
7.   *Méjico produce los cereales, los cultivos tropicales, el petróleo y el gas natural.*
8.   *El idioma oficial de Méjico es el español.*
9.   *Su moneda es el peso mexicano.*
10. *Tienes que visitar las famosas Pirámides de Teotihuacán.*

Exercise 5.20
Pupil's Book: Page 122.

This exercise allows the whole area of stereotypes to be discussed, while providing valuable practice with nationalities and personal descriptions. Those using the CD Rom can click on each picture to hear the descriptions that follow. These were recorded at the end of a recording session by two Spanish girls, without any form of script. We then found pictures to match the descriptions.

Ejemplo: Los españoles son todos bajos y morenos y tocan la guitarra

1.   *Los americanos son muy patrióticos. .*
2.   *Los holandeses son tan simpaticos.*
3.   *Los chinos son tímidos y hay muchos.*
4.   *Los ingleses son bastante educados, los ingleses son muy divertidos.*
5.   *Los escoceses llevan faldas muy divertidas.*
6.   *Los egipcios viven en pirámides muy antiguas.*
7.   *A los franceses les gusta comer muy bien y a veces llevan unos gorros muy divertidos.*
8.   *A los australianos les gusta mucho la playa y creo que también la cerveza y también el surf.*

Translations:

Ejemplo: The Spanish are all short and dark and play the guitar.

1.   The Americans are very patriotic.
2.   The Dutch are so friendly.
3.   The Chinese are shy and there are lots of them.
4.   The English are quite polite; the English are very funny.
5.   The Scots wear very funny kilts.
6.   The Egyptians live in very old pyramids.
7.   The French like to eat very well and sometimes they wear very funny berets.
8.   The Australians really like the beach and I think also beer and also surf.

Exercise 5.21
Pupil's Book: Page 122.

1. *El es de Bogotá. Es colombiano.*
2. *Ella es de Oporto. Es portuguesa.*
3. *Nosotros somos ingleses. Somos de Londres.*
4. *Las chicas son americanas. Son de California.*
5. *¿De dónde es?*
6. *¿De dónde son?*
7. *Tú eres de Francia, ¿no?*
8. *Yo soy de Rusia. Soy rusa.*

Those using the CD Rom can display the translations by clicking on the Spanish flag icons.

El Tiempo
Pupil's Book: Page 123.

This section allows pupils to learn the main phrases used to describe the weather. It allows the verb *hacer* to be revised (Unit 3 page 69). Some pupils will enjoy discussing the glorious subject of apocopation in phrases such as *buen tiempo* and *mal tiempo*, others will not!

Exercise 5.22
Pupil's Book: Page 123; Audio track: 51

In this exercise, pupils listen to the weather forecast for 4th April and then fill in the gaps in the sentences that follow.

Audio CD 2 Track 51:

"Hoy, día 4 de abril, hace bastante mal tiempo en toda la península, excepto en el sur del país, donde hace un tiempo muy soleado con una máxima de 18 grados. En Galicia y Asturias hay fuertes chubascos acompañados de vientos fuertes y las temperaturas sólo alcanzan los 10 grados. En Cataluña y el País Vasco también hay tiempo lluvioso con algunos claros por la tarde. En el centro del país también hay precipitaciones muy fuertes. ¡Hoy desde luego hay que sacar los paraguas!"

Translation:

Today, the 4th April, it is quite bad weather in the whole peninsula, except in the south of the country, where it is very sunny with a maximum temperature of 18°. In Galicia and Asturias there are heavy showers accompanied by strong winds and temperatures only reaching 10°. In Catalonia and in the Basque Country there is also rainy weather with some clear patches in the afternoon. In the centre of the country also there is very heavy rain. Today of course you need to get out your umbrellas!

Answers (in bold):

1. *Hoy es el **4** de **abril.***
2. *Hace bastante **mal** tiempo en España excepto en el **sur.***
3. *Allí hace un tiempo **muy soleado.***
4. *La temperatura máxima es de **18** grados.*
5. *En Galicia y Asturias hay f**uertes chubascos acompañados de vientos fuertes.***
6. *En el centro de España **llueve** mucho.*
7. *Tienes que sacar el **paraguas**.*

Those using the CD Rom can fill in the gaps on the screen by clicking on the **?** icons.

Exercise 5.23
Pupil's Book: Page 124; Audio track: 52

In this screen pupils listen to a description of the climate in Spain and then have to mark the statements that follow as true or false.

Audio CD 2 Track 52:

"En Andalucía en verano hace muy buen tiempo. Hace mucho calor y mucho sol. A veces la temperatura alcanza hasta los 40º grados. Llueve muy poco y la tierra está muy seca, y muchas veces hay tormentas. En la costa hay muchos turistas extranjeros especialmente en Málaga y Marbella, porque les gusta mucho bañarse en el mar y tomar el sol."

Translation:

In Andalucía in Summer the weather is very good. It is very hot and very sunny. Sometimes the temperature even reaches 40 degrees. It rains very little and the ground is very dry and very often there are storms. On the coast there are many foreign tourists, especially in Málaga and Marbella, because they really like to bathe in the sea and enjoy the sun.

Answers:

1. In Andalucia in Summer it is very cold. (False)
2. It is very sunny. (True)
3. Sometimes the temperature reaches 50º. (False)
4. It hardly rains. (True)
5. There are never any storms. (False)
6. The foreign tourists like the climate in Málaga. (True)

Exercise 5.24
Pupil's Book: Page 124; Audio track: 53

In this exercise, pupils listen to the conversation between a foreign male tourist and a local woman. They then answer the questions that follow.

Audio CD 2 Track 53:

Extranjero: *Buenas tardes, señora. Me gustaría saber un poco sobre el clima en Galicia en otoño.*

Señora: *Pues aquí normalmente hace un tiempo bastante bueno y agradable en esta región. A veces llueve bastante pero no hace mucho frío.*

Extranjero: *¿Hace sol todos los días como en el sur?*

Señora: *¡Pues la verdad, no! Hay días nublados y grises y a veces hace un poco de viento, pero normalmente el otoño es bastante suave.*

Extranjero: *Muchas gracias, señora.*

Señora: *De nada, señor. Adiós.*

Extranjero: *Adiós.*

Translation:

Un Extranjero: Good afternoon, sir. I would like to know a little about the climate in Galicia in Autumn.

Una señora: Well, normally here the weather is quite good and pleasant in this region. Sometimes it rains a bit but it isn't very cold.

Extranjero:	Is it sunny every day like in the south?
Señora:	Well to tell the truth, no. There are cloudy, grey days and sometimes there is a little wind, but normally in Autumn it is quite mild.
Extranjero:	Many thanks, madam.
Señora:	Not at all, sir. Goodbye.
Extranjero:	Goodbye.

Answers:

1. What is the weather like normally in Galicia in Autumn.
    Normalmente hace un tiempo bastante bueno y agradable.
    Normally the weather is quite good and pleasant

2. Does it rain?
    A veces llueve bastante.
    Sometimes it rains quite a lot.

3. Is it cold?
    No hace mucho frío.
    It isn't very cold.

4. Is the climate the same as in the south? Why (not)?
    No. Hay días nublados y grises y a veces hace un poco de viento.
    No. There are cloudy, grey days and sometimes there is a little wind.

5. In general, what is the climate like in Galicia in this season of the year?
    Normalmente el otoño es bastante suave.
    Normally in Autumn it is quite mild.

Exercise 5.25
Pupil's Book: Page 125; Audio track: 54

In this exercise we hear two women discussing the weather in Madrid. Pupils than have to paraphrase the material.

Those using the CD Rom can translate the passage on the screen by clicking on the Union Flag icons.

Audio CD 2 Track 54:

La señora A:	*¡Ay, qué frío hace esta mañana! Estamos a 2 grados nada más. Tengo las manos heladas.*
La Señora B:	*Yo también… pues el hombre del tiempo dice que a lo mejor nieva este fin de semana…*
La señora A:	*No creo, pero en la Sierra seguro que sí. Para la gente a la que le gusta esquiar hace un tiempo perfecto, ¿no?*
La Señora B:	*Lo bueno es que aquí en Madrid hace bastante sol en invierno, no como en el norte donde siempre está nublado. Aquí normalmente tenemos un cielo azul, ¿verdad?*
La señora A:	*Pues sí, es verdad pero ¡mucho frío, sí que hace!*
La Señora B:	*Yo de todas formas prefiero el verano.*

Translation:

La señora A: Oh, how cold it is this morning. We are 2 degrees, no more. My hands are frozen.

La Señora B: Me too. Well the weather man says that it will probably snow this weekend...

La señora A: I don't think so, but in the mountains, yes for sure. For people who like skiing it is perfect, isn't it?

La señora B: The good thing is that here in Madrid it is quite sunny in winter, not like in the north where it is always cloudy. Here we normally have a blue sky, don't we?

La señora A: Well yes, it is true but very cold, really so!

La señora B: Anyway, I myself prefer the Summer.

Exercise 5.26
Pupil's Book: Page 125.

In this exercise pupils study a weather map, allowing them to discuss the weather. The questions below are displayed as a prompt. Those using the CD Rom can display the suggested answers by clicking on the **?** icons.

1.   What is the weather like in Barcelona?
2.   Is it raining in Seville?
3.   Where is it snowing?
4.   What is the temperature in Madrid?
5.   What is the weather in the north/south/east/west?

Answers:

1.   *En Barcelona hace sol y está nublado*
2.   *No, no llueve en Sevilla*
3.   *Nieva en los Pirineos*
4.   *En Madrid la temperatura es de 17∞*
5.   *En el Norte llueve en la Cordillera Cantábrica.*
        En el Sur hace sol.
        En el Este hace sol y está nublado.
        En el Oeste hace sol y está nublado.

Exercise 5.27
Pupil's Book: Page 126.

This exercise allows pupils to read a more detailed description of the weather in Spain, season by season. They then answer the questions that follow.

Translation:

In Spain the climate is very varied and the weather in the north, for example in Galicia and in Asturias, is very different from the weather in the south, that is in Andalucía.

In winter it is very cold in some parts of the country, particularly in the Pyrenees, Sierra Nevada and the Picos de Europa where it usually snows quite a lot. For that reason skiing is a very popular sport in these mountains. But in the southern part, especially on the coast, it is usually a pleasant temperature – around 14° – and it is sunny. In the centre of the country in Castille the temperatures are very low, sometimes 0° but normally the sky is blue and the days sunny.

In Spring it rains quite a lot in many parts of the peninsula, especially in the north and for that reason the countryside is very green. Sometimes it is windy and a little cool.

Nevertheless in summer the weather is very good in the whole country. It is very hot, it almost never rains and the skies are almost always clear. The temperatures usually reach around 30º in the south but sometimes there are storms. The people go to the beach to swim and to cool down!

The Autumn is a very pleasant season in Spain. The temperatures are milder than in summer and the days are shorter. Sometimes it is cloudy and it rains but as a general rule there is no bad weather. How nice!

Suggested answers:

1. What is the climate like in Spain?
   En España el clima es muy variado.
   In Spain the climate is very varied.

2. Where is it very cold in winter?
   En invierno hace mucho frío en los Pirineos, Sierra Nevada y los Picos de Europa.
   In winter it is very cold in the Pyrenees, Sierra Nevada and the Picos de Europa.

3. Why is skiing popular?
   El esquí es popular porque en la sierra suele nevar bastante.
   Skiing is popular because in the mountains it usually snows quite a lot.

4. Does it snow in winter on the coasts of the south of Spain?
   No. En las costas del sur en invierno suele hacer una temperatura agradable.
   No. On the coasts of the south the weather is usually mild in winter.

5. What is the weather like in the south in winter?
   Hace agradable, unos 14 grados – y hace sol.
   It is mild, around 14 degrees – and it is sunny.

6. When does it rain in Spain?
   En España suele llover en primavera y a veces en otoño.
   In Spain it usually rains in Spring and sometimes in the Autumn.

7. When is it hot?
   Hace calor en verano.
   It is hot in summer.

8. What do the people do in summer? Why?
   La gente va a la playa a bañarse y refrescarse!
   The people go to the beach to swim and cool down.

9. What is Autumn like in Spain?
   El otoño es muy agradable en España. Las temperaturas son más suaves que en verano y los días son más cortos. A veces está nublado y llueve pero por regla general no hace mal tiempo.
   The Autumn is very pleasant in Spain. The temperatures are milder than in summer and the days are shorter. Sometimes it is cloudy and it rains but as a general rule there is no bad weather.

10. What do you think of the Spanish climate?
    Me gusta el clima español porque, hasta en invierno, normalmente el cielo es azul y los días soleados.
    I like the Spanish climate because, even in Winter, the sky is normally blue and the days are sunny.

Exercise 5.28
Pupil's Book: Page 127.

This exercise allows pupils to practise their written work by writing about the climate in their own country. They may be encouraged to utilise phrases, judiciously altered, from the passage in Exercise 5.27.

UNIT 6: Pasatiempos

About the unit

This final unit gives pupils an opportunity to use the language they have learnt so far to communicate about their hobbies, interests and leisure activities.

New language content:

- *gustar, preferir* + infinitive
- present continuous tense
- modal verbs *poder, querer*
- interjections
- subject pronouns *él, ella, usted*
- *ir a* + infinitive (immediate future)

New contexts:

- leisure, hobbies, sport, music
- family activities

This unit is expected to take 12–15 hours.

Where the unit fits in

Pupils have already learnt how to talk about their routines, places in town and the weather. They consolidate their knowledge and understanding of verbs and extend this to talking about what they are going to do using the immediate future. Reading skills are extended, as is the use of ICT.

Expectations

At the end of this unit most pupils will: read short texts about leisure activities, deducing meanings and using a dictionary where necessary; understand information about future plans from passages made up of familiar words; say what they are doing at the moment, what they are going to do, and describe what other people are doing; speak with reasonably accurate pronunciation and intonation; speak and write about what leisure activities they like and dislike, giving reasons.

Some pupils will not have made so much progress and will: understand simple phrases about leisure activities and future plans; understand what people are doing from a short written or spoken passage; talk simply about activities they like and dislike doing; say what they are going to do in response to a set question, with visual stimuli; write short sentences about their plans, with help.

Some pupils will have progressed further and will: understand longer passages and conversations, deducing the meaning of new words; note down the main points of spoken or written passages, including a range of tourist materials; take part in structured conversations about plans for the weekend, showing some creativity and fluency; write about their leisure interests, enhancing the language with suitable adverbs and adjectives; use a dictionary and other reference materials to check accuracy and understanding; write paragraphs, largely from memorised language, but incorporating language from different contexts.

JUGAR (ue) / PRACTICAR
Pupil's Book: Page 131.

Teachers may wish to ask pupils to write out the verbs *jugar (ue)* and *practicar* before beginning this unit, as they will be using them frequently in the exercises that follow.

Exercise 6.1
Pupil's Book: Page 131; Audio CD 2 track: 55

In this exercise pupils hear Juan discussing his family and friend David, and their various sporting activities. They then have to match up the correct sports (A-G) with the characters (1-5).

Audio CD 2 Track 55:

Me llamo Juan y juego al baloncesto. Mi amigo David practica la vela. Mi hermana María practica el atletismo. Mis padres son deportistas también. Mi padre, que se llama Antonio practica el ciclismo y mi madre, Marisa, juega al squash.

Translation

My name is Juan and I play basketball. My friend David goes sailing. My sister María does athletics. My parents are also sporty. My father, who is called Antonio, goes cycling and my mother, Marisa, plays squash.

Answers

1 = F
2 = C
3 = B
4 = D
5 = A

Those using the CD Rom can play the audio track and then drag the sports (A-G) onto the characters (1-5).

Exercise 6.2
Pupil's Book: Page 131.

This exercise allows pupils to practise discussing sports. Before beginning, those using the CD Rom can watch a simple animation in which Juan is discussing sports with his gym teacher, as follows:

Profesor:	*¿Qué deportes practicas?*	Which sports do you do?
Juan:	*Practico el atletismo y el fútbol.*	I do athletics and football.
Profesor:	*¿Cuándo juegas al fútbol?*	When do you play football?
Juan:	*Juego al fútbol después del colegio.*	I play football after school.
Profesor:	*¿Cuándo juegas al tenis?*	When do you play tennis?
Juan:	*Juego al tenis los fines de semana.*	I play tennis at the weekends.
Profesor:	*¿Dónde juegas?*	Where do you play?
Juan:	*Juego en la casa de mi amigo.*	I play at my friend's house.
Profesor:	*¿Con quién juegas?*	Who do you play with?
Juan:	*Juego con mis amigos.*	I play with my friends.
Profesor:	*¿Qué deportes te gustan más?*	Which sports do you like most?
Juan:	*Prefiero la vela y el ciclismo.*	I prefer sailing and cycling.

Profesor:	*¿Hay algún deporte que no te gusta?*	Is there any sport that you do not like?
	¿Por qué?	Why?
Juan:	*No me gusta el baloncesto porque*	I don't like basketball because it is very
	es muy difícil.	difficult.

Exercise 6.3
Pupil's Book: Page 131.

In this exercise, pupils rearrange the words to make a sensible phrase, using everything in the box, as in the example.

Suggested answers

1. *A Francisco no le gusta nada ni el ciclismo ni la natación.*
   Franciso does not like either cycling or swimming at all.

2. *¿Dónde y con quién suele David jugar al squash?*
   Where and with whom does David usually play squash?

3. *¿Por qué a José le gusta mucho la vela?*
   Why does José really like sailing?

Exercise 6.4
Pupil's Book: Page 132; Audio CD 2 track: 56

This exercise allows pupils to hear five audio clips. Pupils then answer the questions that follow (which should produce the original statements 1-5).

Audio CD 2 Track 56:

1. *Verónica siempre practica la vela los fines de semana.*
2. *José juega al fútbol con poca frecuencia.*
3. *De vez en cuando Dolores juega al baloncesto.*
4. *Los lunes Juan y Dolores practican la gimnasia, los miércoles juegan al squash.*
5. *Los sábados los chicos juegan al rugby y las chicas juegan al fútbol.*

Translation/answers:

1. Veronica always goes sailing at the weekends.
2. José rarely plays football.
3. Sometimes Dolores plays basketball.
4. Juan and Dolores do gym on Mondays, and on Wednesdays they play squash.
5. On Saturdays the boys play rugby and the girls play football.

Those using the CD Rom can display the answers by clicking on the **?** icons.

Los pasatiempos
Pupil's Book: Page 132.

Those using the CD Rom can see four simple animations in which the character say the following phrases:

1. *No me gusta la lectura.* — I don't like reading.
2. *No me gusta nada el teatro.* — I don't like the theatre at all.
3. *No me gusta mucho la música clásica.* — I don't much like classical music.
4. *¡Prefiero la música pop!* — I prefer pop music!

This acts as useful practice before they attempt Exercise 6.5.

Exercise 6.5
Pupil's Book: Page 132.

In this exercise, pupils have to rearrange the words in the jumbled sentences in the correct order so that they make sense:

Answers:

1. *A José no le gusta la lectura.*
    José does not like reading.

2. *A Victoria le gusta la música pop.*
    Victoria likes pop music.

3. *A Juan no le gusta nada el teatro.*
    Juan does not like the theatre at all.

4. *A Dolores no le gusta mucho la música clásica.*
    Dolores does not like classical music much.

Exercise 6.6
Pupil's Book: Page 132; Audio tracks: 57-61

In this exercise, pupils listen to five characters discussing their likes and dislikes with their teacher with regard to sports and passtimes. Pupils should copy and fill in the table. Teachers can decide whether they wish pupils to note down only those things which the characters really like or really do not like (in keeping with the two happy/sad faces in the table), or whether all likes and dislikes should be included.

Audio CD 2 Track 57:

Profesora: *Hola, Lolita. ¿Qué deportes practicas?*

Loita: *Pues, juego al baloncesto y al tenis pero lo que más me gusta es la natación. Voy a la piscina todos los días antes del colegio. No me gusta mucho la gimnasia.*

Profesora: *¿Tienes algún otro pasatiempo?*

Loita: *Sí, me encanta la lectura – leo sobre todo libros de aventuras.*

Translation:

Profesora: Hello Lolita. What sports do you do?

Loita: Well, I play basketball and tennis but the thing I like best is swimming. I go to the swimming pool every day before school. I don't like gym much.

Profesora: Do you have any other hobby?

Loita: Yes, I love reading – I read especially adventure books.

Audio CD 2 Track 58:

Profesora: *¿Qué hay, Eduardo? ¿Qué deportes practicas normalmente?*

Eduardo: *Pues, en el cole juego al fútbol y al voleibol pero el deporte que más me gusta es el esquí. Vivimos cerca de los Pirineos así que suelo esquiar bastante en invierno con mis amigos.*

Profesora: *¿Te gusta la natación?*

Eduardo: *No mucho. Prefiero montar en bicicleta.*

Translation:

Profesora:	How are you doing, Eduardo? What hobbies do you do normally?
Eduardo:	Well, at school I play football and volleyball but the sport I like best is skiing. We live near the Pyrenees so I usually ski quite a lot in winter with my friends.
Profesora:	Do you like swimming?
Eduardo:	Not much. I prefer going bicycling.

Audio CD 2 Track 59:

Profesora:	*Hola, Felipe. ¿Te gustan los deportes?*
Felipe:	*Pues no me gustan nada (porque se me da fatal jugar) el fútbol y el baloncesto en el colegio, pero la vela sí me gusta.*
Profesora:	*Entonces, ¿Qué otra cosa haces con tu tiempo libre?*
Felipe:	*Toco la guitarra. Me encanta la música.*
Profesora:	*¿Te gusta la música clásica?*
Felipe:	*No, nada. Prefiero la música pop.*

Translation:

Profesora:	Hello Felipe. Do you like sports?
Felipe:	Well, I really don't like (because I am useless at playing) football and basketball at school, but I do like sailing.
Profesora:	Then, what else do you do with your free time?
Felipe:	I play the guitar. I love music.
Profesora:	Do you like classical music?
Felipe:	No, not at all. I prefer pop music.

Audio CD 2 Track 60:

Profesora:	*¿Y tú, Cristina? ¿Qué deportes te gustan?*
Cristina:	*Pues hago gimnasia y baloncesto en el colegio pero no me gustan mucho. Pero soy miembro de un club de atletismo y eso sí que me gusta mucho.*
Profesora:	*¿Tienes algún otro pasatiempo?*
Cristina:	*Pues, me gusta bailar y escuchar música.*

Translation:

Profesora:	And you, Cristina, what sports do you like?
Cristina:	Well, I do gym and basketball at school, but I don't like them much. But I am a member of an athletics club and so I really like that.
Profesora:	Do you have any other hobby?
Cristina:	Well, I like dancing and listening to music.

Audio CD 2 Track 61:

Profesora:	*Hola, Elena. ¿Qué deportes practicas?*

Elena:	Pues hago patinaje, que me gusta mucho y luego como vivo cerca del mar practico deportes acuáticos como el windsurfing. En el colegio hacemos gimnasia que se me da muy bien y también jugamos al tenis. Soy bastante deportista, entonces me gustan todos los deportes.
Profesora:	¿Y aparte de los deportes…?
Elena:	Me gusta mucho la discoteca, sí, ir con mis amigas a la discoteca.

Translation:

Profesora:	Hello Elena. Which sports do you do?
Elena:	Well I do skating, which I really like, and then as I live near the sea I do aquatic sports such as windsurfing. At school we do gym which I'm very good at and we also play tennis. I am quite sporty, so I like all sports.
Profesora:	And apart from sports?
Elena:	I really like the disco, yes, to go with my girlfriends to the disco.

Answers

(Those that are really liked or really disliked are shown in bold.)

Nombre	☺☺	☹☹
Lolita	baloncesto, tenis, **natación, lectura**	–
Eduardo	fútbol, voleibol, **esquí,ciclismo**	natación
Felipe	vela, **guitarra, música pop**	**fútbol, baloncesto**, música clásica
Cristina	**atletismo, bailar, música**	gimnasia, baloncesto
Elena	**patinaje**, windsurfing, gimnasia, tenis, **discoteca**	–

Those using the CD Rom can display the answers on the screen by clicking on the **?** icons.

Exercise 6.7
Pupil's Book: Page 133; Audio CD 2 track: 62

In this exercise, pupils read and/or listen to the passage on the Martínez family and answer the questions that follow.

Audio CD 2 Track 62:

La familia Martínez

En esta familia hay 5 personas y todos son muy deportistas. El padre, que se llama Carlos, es un hombre muy activo – en verano después del trabajo juega al tenis tres veces por semana en el club de tenis de Tarragona. Es su deporte favorito y se le da bastante bien. En invierno suele hacer footing para mantenerse en forma.

Su mujer, Carmen, es profesora de guitarra y va a clase de gimnasia con sus amigas los lunes, los miércoles y los viernes. A veces acompaña a su marido a hacer footing.

Sus tres hijos – Susana, Maribel y Daniel – van al mismo colegio donde practican la gimnasia, el atletismo y el baloncesto. A Daniel le gusta mucho el baloncesto y juega para el equipo del colegio. A las dos hermanas les gusta mucho la natación pero no hay piscina en el colegio por lo que tienen que ir a un polideportivo en el centro del pueblo. Son muy buenas nadadoras.

Los fines de semana, cuando hace buen tiempo, todos van al mar a practicar la vela.

Translation:

The Martínez family

In this family there are 5 people and they are all very sporty. The father, who is called Carlos, is a very active man – in summer after work he plays tennis three times per week at the tennis club in Tarragona. It is his favourite sport and he is quite good. In winter he usually goes jogging to keep fit.

His wife, Carmen, is a guitar teacher and goes to a gym class with her girlfriends on Mondays, Wednesdays and Fridays. Sometimes she goes jogging with her husband.

Their three children, Susana, Maribel and Daniel, go to the same school where they do gym, athletics and basketball. Daniel really likes basketball and plays for the school team. His two sisters really like swimming but there is no swimming pool at school so they have to go to a sports centre in the centre of the town. They are very good swimmers.

At the weekends, when the weather is good, they all go to the sea to go sailing.

Answers

1. *Sí, a la familia Martínez le gusta el deporte.*
    Yes, the Martinez family likes sport.

2. *El padre juega al tenis y hace footing.*
    The father plays tennis and goes jogging.

3. *Carmen va a clase de gimnasia los lunes, los miércoles y los viernes.*
    Carmen goes to her gym class on Mondays, Wednesdays and Fridays.

4. *El deporte favorito de Daniel es el baloncesto.*
    Daniel's favourite sport is Basketball.

5. *Susana y Maribel prefieren la natación.*
    Susana and Maribel prefer swimming.

6. *No hay piscina en el colegio.*
    There is no swimming pool in the school.

7. *Van a un polideportivo en el centro del pueblo.*
    They go to a sports centre in the centre of the town.

8. *Van al mar a practicar la vela.*
    They go to the seaside to go sailing.

Those using the CD Rom can display the translation of each paragraph by clicking on the Union Flag icons, and then display the answer to the questions by clicking on the **?** icons.

Exercise 6.8
Pupil's Book: Page 134.

In this exercises, pupils have to rearrange the words in the correct order.

1.	*José juega al fútbol.*	José plays football.
2.	*Felipe practica el atletismo cada día.*	Felipe does athletics every day.
3.	*Las chicas guapas siempre juegan al baloncesto.*	The pretty girls always play basketball.
4.	*Los chicos inteligentes nunca juegan al fútbol.*	The intelligent boys never play football.
5.	*En España nosotros jugamos al golf los fines de semana.*	In Spain we play golf at the weekends.

Exercise 6.9
Pupil's Book: Page 134.

1. *Mi hermano juega al rugby los fines de semana.*
2. *Mis amigos siempre juegan al baloncesto los domingos.*
3. *Mi hermana suele practicar el atletismo los martes.*
4. *Nosotros nunca jugamos al fútbol en el colegio.*
5. *Mi padre juega a veces al squash después del trabajo.*

Those using the CD Rom may display the translations by clicking on the Spanish flag icons.

¿Qué prefieres hacer?
Pupil's Book: Page 134.

This exercise allows pupils to practise talking about their passtimes and hobbies, using a wider range of vocabulary.

Exercise 6.10
Pupil's Book: Page 135.

1. I really like going to festivals on Saturdays.
2. I love chatting with my friends on the telephone.
3. I really don't like writing letters.
4. I prefer sending e-mails.
5. I like skiing in the Pyrenees because it's cool.
6. Do you like going shopping?
7. My father likes playing golf.
8. My mother likes watching soap operas.
9. I like having a great time!
10. We prefer football to tennis.

Those using the CD Rom may display the translations by clicking on the Union Flag icons.

Exercise 6.11
Pupil's Book: Page 135.

In this exercise pupils practise talking about their free time, giving reasons for their likes and dislikes. Those using the CD Rom can watch a simple animation in which Carolina tells the Profesora what she does in her free time.

Profesora: *¿Qué te gusta hacer en tus ratos libres?*

Carolina: *Me gusta practicar la vela o ir al cine, pero no me gusta nadar.*

Profesora: *¿Qué prefieres hacer?*

Carolina: *Creo que prefiero practicar la vela.*

Profesora: *¿Por qué?*

Carolina: *Porque me encanta; ¡es divertido!*

Exercise 6.12
Pupil's Book: Page 135.

This screen displays the correct translations.

1. *¿Qué te gusta hacer en tus ratos libres?"*
2. *Me gusta practicar la natación y bailar.*
3. *A ella le gusta leer.*
4. *Nos gustan los deportes acuáticos.*
5. *Prefieren ir a la discoteca.*

Exercise 6.13
Pupil's Book: Page 136.

In this exercise, pupils have to create sentences using the words and phrases from the four columns. For example they might create:

A veces me gusta salir con amigos.

Those using the CD Rom can drag the words and phrases around the screen to build the sentences.

Exercise 6.14
Pupil's Book: Page 136.

In this exercise, pupils are revising the use of *me gusta* and have to fill in the gaps in the chewed letter from Carlos.

The missing words are shown below in bold.

*Me llamo **Carlos** y voy a hablar de*
mi familia y de mis amigos. A mí me
gustan** mucho los deportes. Sobre todo **me
*gusta la natación, pero no me **gusta***
el rugby. ¡Es una barbaridad! A mis padres
***les** gusta mucho ir a los toros*
*pero a mi hermano, Imanol, no **le***
gusta la corrida. Tengo muchos amigos.
*Mi mejor amiga se llama Carolina y **le***
*gusta mucho bailar en la disco. A **mí***
me gusta bailar también. Tengo un
amigo que se llama Manuel. A Manuel le
***gusta** practicar la vela. A mi no me*
gustan** los deportes acuáticos. ¿Qué **te
gusta hacer en tu tiempo libre?

¡Escríbeme pronto!

Saludos de Carlos

Translation:

My name is Carlos and I am going to talk about my family and my friends. I really like sport. I particularly like swimming, but I don't like rugby. It is barbaric! My parents really like going to bull fights but my brother Imanol doesn't like bullfighting. I have lots of friends. My best friend is called Carolina and she really likes dancing in the disco. I myself also like dancing. I have a friend called Manuel. Manuel likes sailing. I don't like aquatic sports. What do you like doing in your free time?

Write soon!

Best wishes,

from Carlos

Exercise 6.15
Pupil's Book: Page 137; Audio CD 2 tracks: 63-67

In this exercise pupils hear five characters talking about their hobbies. They should copy and complete the table.

Audio CD 2 Track 63:

Profesora:	*Hola Teresa. ¿Qué te gusta hacer en tus ratos libres?*
Teresa:	*Pues me gusta mucho el ciclismo. Normalmente monto en bici los fines de semana y también me encanta ir con mis amigas a la discoteca.*

Profesora:	Hello Teresa. What do you like doing in your free time?
Teresa:	Well I really like cycling. I normally go on my bike at the weekends and I also love going with my friends to the disco.

Audio CD 2 Track 64:

Profesora:	*Hola, José María. ¿Qué prefieres hacer en tu tiempo libre?*
José María:	*Pues, me gustan mucho todos los deportes pero creo que prefiero el fútbol porque juego todos los días. En invierno practico el esquí con mi familia en los Pirineos.*

Profesora:	Hello, José María. What do you prefer doing in your free time?
José María:	Well, I really like all sports but I think I prefer football because I play every day. In winter I go skiing with my family in the Pyrenees.

Audio CD 2 Track 65:

Profesora:	*¿Y tú, Manolo? ¿Qué te gusta hacer en tu tiempo libre?*
Manolo:	*Pues, a mí me encanta el baloncesto. Juego en el colegio los martes y los jueves. Los fines de semana me gusta mucho ir al cine, bailar y ¡pasarlo bomba!*

Profesora:	And you, Manolo? What do you like doing in your free time?
Manolo:	Well, I love basketball. I play in school on Tuesdays and Thursdays. At the weekends I really love going to the cinema, dancing and having a great time!

Audio CD 2 Track 66:

Profesora:	*Hola Laura. En tus ratos libres, ¿qué te gusta hacer?*
Laura:	*Lo que me gusta mucho es la tele. ¡Me chiflan las telenovelas! Suelo verlas por la tarde después del colegio. Los sábados me gusta mucho ir de tiendas con mis amigas y luego a una cafetería a tomar una coca cola. Por la tarde a veces voy al teatro con mis padres o a casa de una amiga.*

Profesora:	Hello Laura. In your free time, what do you like doing?
Laura:	The thing I really like is TV. I love soap operas. I usually watch them in the afternoon after school. On Saturdays I really like going shopping with my friends and then to a cafe to have a coco cola. In the evening I sometimes go to the theatre with my parents or go home with a friend.

Audio CD 2 Track 67:

Profesora:	*¿Y tú, Elena? ¿Qué sueles hacer en tus ratos libres?*
Elena:	*Pues creo que lo que más me gusta es la natación. Voy a la piscina a nadar todos los días a las siete de la mañana. También me gusta relajarme, leer revistas y navegar por Internet. ¡Me encanta mi tiempo libre!*

Profesora:	And you, Elena? What do you usually do in your free time?
Elena:	Well I think the thing I like best is swimming. I go to the swimming pool to swim every day at 7.00 in the morning. I also like chilling out, reading magazines and surfing the internet. I love my free time!

Answers:

Nombre	☺ ¿Qué les gusta?	¿Cuándo?
1. **Teresa**	el ciclismo, la discoteca	los fines de semana
2. **José María**	el fútbol	todos los días
	el esquí	en invierno
3. **Manolo**	el baloncesto	los martes y los jueves
	ir al cine, bailar y pasarlo bomba	los fines de semana
4. **Laura**	la tele	por la tarde después del colegio
	ir de tiendas/ir a una cafetería	los sábados
	el teatro/casa de una amiga	a veces por la tarde
5. **Elena**	la natación	todos los días a la siete.
	relajarse, leer revistas, navegar por Internet	ratos libres

The present continuous tense
Pupil's Book: Page 138.

Pupils should be encouraged to master the formation of the present participle for the various conjugations. Particular care needs to be taken with AR verbs so that an extra *i* does not creep in (eg *estudiando* only goes *iando* because the stem of *estudiar* ends in an *i*). Once this has been achieved, using this tense is very simple. Students of Latin may wish to discuss the similarity between *el gerundio* in Spanish and the gerund in Latin.

En Casa
Pupil's Book: Page 139; Audio CD 2 track: 68

This passage can be read and/or listened to and provides practice at the present continuous tense. The mother is trying to get her family to help her in the kitchen. Each member of the family has an excuse...

Audio CD 2 Track 68:

Mamá:	*"¿Me ayudas en la cocina, por favor, Pablo?"*
Pablo:	*"Pero mamá, estoy estudiando. Tengo un examen mañana...."*
Mamá:	*"Niñas, ¿qué estáis haciendo?"*
Niñas:	*"Estamos viendo un programa muy interesante en la tele..."*
Mamá:	*"¿Y papá, qué está haciendo?"*
Ana:	*"Creo que está leyendo un libro en el salón..."*
Mamá:	*"¡Vaya familia!"*

Translation:

Mamá:	Will you help me in the kitchen, please, Pablo?
Pablo:	But mum, I am studying. I have an exam tomorrow...
Mamá:	Girls, what are you doing?
Niñas:	We are watching a very interesting programme on the TV...
Mamá:	And what is Dad doing?
Ana:	I think he is reading a book in the sitting room...
Mamá:	What a family!

Exercise 6.16
Pupil's Book: Page 139.

1. The girl is writing a letter.
2. The man is working in an office.
3. The tourists are visiting the cathedral.
4. The boys are watching the television.
5. The girls are listening to music.

Those using the CD Rom can display the translations by clicking on the Union Flag icons.

Exercise 6.17
Pupil's Book: Page 139.

1.	*fumar*	*fumando*
2.	*comer*	*comiendo*
3.	*vivir*	*viviendo*
4.	*nadar*	*nadando*
5.	*beber*	*bebiendo*

Those using the CD Rom can display the answers by clicking on the **?** icons.

Exercise 6.18

¡Escribe!

1. *El profesor está hablando en español.*
2. *Los chicos están comiendo chocolate en el salón.*
3. *¿Qué estás haciendo?*
4. *Estamos escribiendo un ejercicio en inglés.*
5. *Estoy escuchando la radio en mi dormitorio.*

Those using the CD Rom can display the translations by clicking on the Spanish flag icons.

Exercise 6.19
Pupil's Book: Page 140.

This exercise provides vital practice at forming the present continuous tense of reflexive verbs.

1. *ducharse*

me estoy duchando	or	*estoy duchándome*	I am showering , etc.
te estás duchando		*estás duchándote*	
se está duchando		*está duchándose*	
nos estamos duchando		*estamos duchándonos*	
os estáis duchando		*estáis duchándoos*	
se están duchando		*están duchándose*	

2. *levantarse*

me estoy levantando	or	*estoy levantándome*	I am getting up, etc.
te estás levantando		*estás levantándote*	
se está levantando		*está levantándose*	
nos estamos levantando		*estamos levantándonos*	
os estáis levantando		*estáis levantándoos*	
se están levantando		*están levantándose*	

Those using the CD Rom can display this information by clicking on the **?** icons.

Exercise 6.20
Pupil's Book: Page 140.

In this exercise pupils first identify all the reflexive verbs, then rewrite these in the alternative form, and then translate the phrase that they are part of.

Translation:

It is 7.30 in the morning. Mr Muñoz is getting ready for work – he is washing and shaving while his wife is combing her hair in the bedroom. Miguel, the older son is getting out of bed but is very sleepy. His sister, Carolina, is getting ready for school; so she is having a shower in the bathroom. Ángel is waking up very slowly – because he doesn't much like going to school!

Answers:

The following phrases should be identified and manipulated as directed:

1. *está arreglándose > se está arreglando*
   He is getting ready.
2. *está lavándose y afeitándose > se está lavando y afeitando*
   He is washing and shaving.
3. *se está peinando > está peinándose*
   She is combing her hair.
4. *está levantándose > se está levantando*
   He is getting up.
5. *está preparándose > se está preparando*
   She is getting ready.
6. *se está duchando > está duchándose*
   She is having a shower.
7. *se está despertando > está despertándose*
   He is waking up.

Those using the CD Rom can display the passage on the screen, underline the reflexive verbs (1), write these in both forms (2), and then translate them (3), by clicking on the buttons numbered 1-3. The passage itself can also be heard by clicking on the red audio player.

Exercise 6.21
Pupil's Book: Page 141.

1. I am beginning to read a very interesting book.
2. What are you thinking?
3. The children are playing in the park.
4. At this moment my father is returning from the office.
5. We are going to bed because we are sleepy.

Those using the CD Rom can display the translations by clicking on the Union Flag icons.

Exercise 6.22
Pupil's Book: Page 141.

1. What are you doing?
2. I am getting dressed in my bedroom.
3. What is Juan doing?
4. He is sleeping on the sofa.

Those using the CD Rom can display the translations by clicking on the Union Flag icons.

Exercise 6.23
Pupil's Book: Page 141.

Pupils may need to be reminded that *vestirse (i)*, being reflexive, will have two forms, both of which should be written out.

1. *empezar (ie)*

	Singular	**Plural**
1st person	*Estoy empezando*	*Estamos empezando*
2nd person	*Estás empezando*	*Estáis empezando*
3rd person	*Está empezando*	*Están empezando*

2. *jugar (ue)*

	Singular	**Plural**
1st person	*Estoy jugando*	*Estamos jugando*
2nd person	*Estás jugando*	*Estáis jugando*
3rd person	*Está jugando*	*Están jugando*

3. *vestirse (i)*

	Singular	**Plural**
1st person	*me estoy vistiendo*	*nos estamos vistiendo*
2nd person	*te estás vistiendo*	*os estáis vistiendo*
3rd person	*se está vistiendo*	*se están vistiendo*

or

1st person	*estoy vistiéndome*	*estamos vistiéndonos*
2nd person	*estás vistiéndote*	*estáis vistiéndoos*
3rd person	*está vistiéndose*	*están vistiéndose*

4. *dormir (ue)*

	Singular	**Plural**
1st person	*Estoy durmiendo*	*Estamos durmiendo*
2nd person	*Estás durmiendo*	*Estáis durmiendo*
3rd person	*Está durmiendo*	*Están durmiendo*

Exercise 6.24
Pupil's Book: Page 142.

In this exercise, pupils may write or describe aloud what they see in the pictures.

Suggested answers:

1. *El rey y la reina están bailando.*
2. *El chico está jugando al baloncesto.*
3. *El chico y la chica están montando en bicicletas.*
4. *El hombre está leyendo el periódico.*
5. *Los padres están cenando.*
6. *El chico está tocando la guitarra.*
7. *El abuelo está escribendo una carta.*
8. *El perro está durmiendo.*
9. *Las chicas están charlando por teléfono.*

Exercise 6.25
Pupil's Book: Page 143; Audio CD 2 tracks: 69-74

In this exercise, Carolina phones around to all of her friends. Pupils have to listen and work out what the various characters are doing.

Audio CD 2 Track 69:

Carolina: *Oye, Jaime, ¿Qué estás haciendo?*
Jaime: *Pues, en este momento estoy haciendo mis deberes de matemáticas. ¡Vaya rollo! Es muy difícil y estoy harto .....*
Carolina: *Pues nada. Te dejo. ¡Hasta mañana!*

Translation:

Carolina: Hey, Jaime, what are you doing?
Jaime: Well, at this moment I am doing my Maths homework. What a bore! It is very difficult and I am fed up...
Carolina: Well never mind. I'll leave you. See you tomorrow!

Audio CD 2 Track 70:

Carolina: *Oye, Javier, ¿Qué estás haciendo?*
Javier: *Pues, ahora mismo estoy cenando – estoy comiendo una hamburguesa con patatas fritas. ¡Está riquísimo!*
Carolina: *Entonces vamos a la discoteca despúes, vale?*
Javier: *Pues, sí..... a las 11.*
Carolina: *Hasta luego!*
Javier: *Adiós.*

Translation:

Carolina: Hey, Javier, what are you doing?
Javier: Well, right now I am having dinner – I am eating a hamburger with chips. It is delicious!
Carolina: Then let's go to the disco afterwards, okay?
Javier: Well, okay...at 11.00 o'clock.
Carolina: See you later.
Javier: Goodbye.

Audio CD 2 Track 71:

Carolina: *Oye, Marisa. ¿Qué estás haciendo?*
Marisa: *Pues, estoy viendo una telenovela muy interesante con mi hermana, pero termina en seguida.*
Carolina: *¿Entonces salimos a las 6?*
Marisa: *Sí, vale. Hasta luego.*
Carolina: *Hasta luego.*

Translation:

Carolina: Hey, Marisa, what are you doing?
Marisa: Well, I am watching a very interesting soap opera with my sister, but it finishes in a moment.
Carolina: Then shall we go out at 6.00?
Marisa: Yes, okay. See you later.
Carolina: See you later.

Audio CD 2 Track 72:

Carolina:	*Oye, Ester. ¿Vamos de compras ahora?*
Ester:	*Ahora no puedo porque estoy preparando la comida para mi familia.*
Carolina:	*Pues, lo siento. Entonces voy con mi amiga Bea .*
Ester:	*Adiós.*
Carolina:	*Adiós.*

Translation:

Carolina:	Hey, Ester. Are you coming shopping now?
Ester:	I can't now because I am preparing lunch for my family.
Carolina:	Well, I'm sorry. Then I'll go with my friend Bea.
Ester:	Goodbye.
Carolina:	Goodbye.

Audio CD 2 Track 73:

Carolina:	*Oye, Miguel. ¿Por qué no salimos?*
Miguel:	*Sí, pero en este momento estoy fregando los platos para mi madre.*
Carolina:	*¡Ay, pobre! Nos vemos más tarde entonces – sobre las 4, ¿vale?*
Miguel:	*De acuerdo….. hasta luego.*

Translation:

Carolina:	Hey, Miguel. Why don't we go out?
Miguel:	Yes, but at the moment I am washing the dishes for my mother.
Carolina:	Oh, poor thing. We'll meet up later then – around 4.00, okay?
Miguel:	Agreed. See you later.

Audio CD 2 Track 74:

Carolina:	*Oye, Concha, ¿Qué estás haciendo?*
Concha:	*Pues, en este momento estoy jugando con el ordenador – estoy navegando por internet para buscar información para mis deberes de historia.*
Carolina:	*Entonces, te veo mañana en el cole. Adiós.*

Translation:

Carolina:	Hey, Concha. What are you doing?
Concha:	Well at this moment I am playing with the computer – I am surfing the internet to find information for my History homework.
Carolina:	Then I'll see you tomorrow at school. Goodbye.

Answers:

1.	*Jaime está haciendo sus deberes.*	Jaime is doing her homework.
2.	*Javier está cenando.*	Javier is having dinner.
3.	*Marisa viendo una telenovela.*	Marisa is watching a soap opera.
4.	*Ester está preparando la comida.*	Ester is preparing lunch.
5.	*Miguel está fregando los platos.*	Miguel is washing the dishes.
6.	*Concha está navegando por internet.*	Concha is surfing the internet.

Those using the CD Rom can display the answers by clicking on the ? icons.

Exercise 6.26
Pupil's Book: Page 143.

In this exercise, pupils practise asking each other what they are doing and formulating appropriate responses. This can be followed by a mime game, in which pupils mime an action and the rest of the class guess what they are doing.

Querer
Pupil's Book: Page 143.

Pupils may need to be reminded that '*qu*' in Spanish is pronounced as a 'k' apart from in the one word, *el squash*, which is pronounced as it is in English.

Exercise 6.27
Pupil's Book: Page 144; Audio CD 2 tracks: 75-79

In this exercise, pupils listen to the five audio clips and match up the statements a-e with the correct characters 1-5.

Audio CD 2 Track 75:

Carolina:	*Oye, Sergio, ¿Qué quieres hacer esta tarde?*
Sergio:	*Pues me gustaría jugar al tenis porque hace muy buen tiempo.*
Carolina:	*¡Genial!"*

Translation:

Carolina:	Hey, Sergio. What do you want to do this afternoon?
Sergio:	Well I would like to play tennis because it is a very nice day.
Carolina:	Great!

Audio CD 2 Track 76:

Carolina:	*Oye, Patricia. ¿Quieres salir esta noche con nosotras?*
Patricia:	*Lo siento. Imposible, porque tengo que cenar con mis abuelos.*
Carolina:	*¡Qué pena!"*

Translation:

Carolina:	Hey, Patricia. Do you want to go out tonight with us?
Patricia:	Sorry. Impossible, because I have to have dinner with my grandparents.
Carolina:	What a pity!

Audio CD 2 Track 77:

Carolina:	*Silvia, ¿Qué quieres hacer esta mañana?*
Silvia:	*Quiero ir de compras contigo, ¿vale?*
Carolina:	*Estupendo. Vamos ahora.*

Translation:

Carolina:	Silvia, what do you want to do this morning?
Silvia:	I want to go shopping with you.
Carolina:	Superb. Let's go now.

Audio CD 2 Track 78:

Carolina:	*Oye, Juanjo. ¿Quieres ir al cine esta noche?*
Juanjo:	*No – me gustaría pero estoy fatal.*
Carolina:	*Ay, lo siento. Que te mejores."*

Translation:

Carolina:	Hey, Juanjo. Do you want to go to the cinema tonight?
Juanjo:	No, I'd like to but I'm feeling awful.
Carolina:	Oh, sorry. Hope you feel better soon.

Audio CD 2 Track 79:

Carolina:	*Oye, Gabriel. ¿Qué quieres hacer esta tarde?*
Gabriel:	*Quiero practicar la vela porque no tengo nada que hacer.*
Carolina:	*A mí también me gustaría ¡Vamos!"*

Translation:

Carolina:	Hey, Gabriel. What do you want to do this afternoon?
Gabriel:	I want to go sailing because I don't have anything to do.
Carolina:	I would like to too. Let's go!

Answers

1. c   2. d   3. a   4. b   5. e

Those using the CD Rom can drag the answers a-e onto the correct question 1-5.

Exercise 6.28
Pupil's Book: Page 144.

1. In the first part of the exercise pupils should write ten things that they want to do at the weekend, giving reasons.
2. a) *Quiero montar en bicicleta.*
    b) *¿Quieres bailar?*
    c) *Quiere salir.*
    d) *Queremos charlar.*
    e) *¿Queréis ir a la fiesta, verdad?*
    f) *Quieren ver la televisión.*
    g) *¿Qué quiere usted hacer?*

Those using the CD Rom can display the translations to part two of the exercise by clicking on the Spanish flag icons.

Exercise 6.29
Pupil's Book: Page 144.

Pepe:	Mum, I want to go to the disco with my friends this Saturday.
Maria:	And I want to go to a party with Beatriz.
Mamá:	And you Pablo; what do you want to do?
Pablo:	Well Dad and I want to go to the stadium to watch Real Madrid.
Mamá:	But don't you want to go to have dinner at your grandmother's house?
Todos:	Please Mum, you're joking!

Those using the CD Rom can listen to the conversation and then display the translations to each part by clicking on the Union Flag icons.

Exercise 6.30
Pupil's Book: Page 145.

1. *No puedo jugar al tenis.*
2. *¿Podéis salir?*
3. *No puede telefonear.*
4. *Podemos cenar en un restaurante.*
5. *Pueden estudiar en la biblioteca.*
6. *Puede usted hacer vela en España.*

Those using the CD Rom can display the translations to each part by clicking on the Spanish flag icons.

Exercise 6.31
Pupil's Book: Page 145.

This exercise allows teachers to revise the subject pronouns first met in unit 2, page 30:

1. *El martes yo voy al colegio, pero usted va al banco.*
2. *El miércoles nosotros salimos pero ellos se quedan en casa.*
3. *El jueves tú juegas al golf y él juega al baloncesto.*
4. *El viernes ella va de tiendas pero vosotros veis la televisión.*

Exercise 6.32
Pupil's Book: Page 145.

This exercise allows pupils to practise their reading skills. The passage could either be translated, or questions on it could be asked to confirm comprehension. Teachers may wish to explain the use of diminutives ending in *-cito / -cita* and the use of *tí* after a preposition.

Málaga, 22nd November

Hi,

How are you? My name is Jorge and I am 14 years old. I am from Málaga and I live with my family in a little village on the outskirts of Málaga. My grandmother also lives with us. There are 5 of us in total: my parents, my sister (who is called Maribel) and me, and my grandmother of course. We live in quite a big house in the country and so we have lots of animals: 2 big dogs (German shepherds), 4 cats and a tortoise. I love animals. Do you like animals?

I am going to talk to you a little about my daily routine and my hobbies. I go to a mixed school in the centre of Málaga so I have to get up quite early, around 7.30, Mondays to Fridays. What time do you normally get up? I usually have a little breakfast: some orange juice and some biscuits. I leave the house at 8.00 and take the bus which drops me off near the school. Lessons begin at 8.30 but I usually chat with my friends in the courtyard before going in. I normally finish lessons at 2.00 in the afternoon but on Wednesday afternoons we have gym, football and basketball lessons so I don't go home until a little after 6.00.

On Saturdays there is no school, thank goodness, and I can get up late. I really like going out with my friends. Sometimes we go to a bar and chat and have a drink; other times we go to the cinema or a disco. In Summer we go to the beach to swim and go windsurfing. Here in Málaga the weather is very good. What is the weather like where you live? This Saturday we are going to go to a pop concert. Excellent!

Well, no more for today. Write to me soon and tell me about your family, your school and your hobbies.

Love from your friend, Manolo

Those using the CD Rom can listen to the letter being read aloud, and can display the translation paragraph by paragraph.

Exercise 6.33
Pupil's Book: Page 145.

In this exercise, pupils reply to Manolo's letter (see Exercise 6.32). The points that pupils must include in their reply to Manolo are:

1. Do they like animals?
2. What time they normally get up?
3. What the weather is like where they live?
4. Information about their family, school and hobbies.

Exercise 6.34
Pupil's Book: Page 146; Audio CD 2 tracks: 80-83

In this exercise, pupils listen to the four characters speaking and then reply true or false to the questions that follow. If the statement is false, they correct it.

Audio CD 2 Track 80

Me llamo Gloria. Tengo 15 años. Vivo en las islas Canarias con mis padres y mi hermana menor. En mi tiempo libre me gusta leer revistas y ver tele-novelas. Soy muy deportista – juego al baloncesto y al tenis. Me encanta la gimnasia y la natación.

My name is Gloria. I am 15 years old. I live in the Canary Islands with my parents and my younger sister. In my free time I like reading magazines and watching soap operas. I am very sporty – I play basketball and tennis. I love gym and swimming.

Audio CD 2 Track 81

Mi nombre es Alberto. Soy de Costa Rica. Tengo 16 años. En mi familia somos 3 hermanos – todos chicos! A mí me gusta mucho tocar la guitarra – me chifla la música pop. Los sábados voy a la discoteca a bailar con mis amigos. A veces voy a conciertos.

My name is Albert. I am from Costa Rica. I am 16 years old. There are three of us children in my family – all boys! I really like playing the guitar – I love pop music. On Saturdays I go to the disco to dance with my friends. Sometimes I go to concerts.

Audio CD 2 Track 82

Me llamo Raquel. Tengo 24 años. Soy española – de Madrid. Tengo una hermana mayor. Yo trabajo como profesora en una escuela primaria. Los fines de semana me gusta ir con amigos a fiestas. ¡Lo pasamos bomba!

My name is Raquel. I am 24 years old. I am Spanish – from Madrid. I have an older sister. I work as a teacher in a primary school. At the weekends I like going to parties with my friends. We have a great time!

Audio CD 2 Track 83

Soy Marcelo. Tengo 14 años. Vivo con mis padres en Buenos Aires, en Argentina. Somos familia numerosa, 3 chicas y 3 chicos. Muchos hermanos, ¿verdad? En mis ratos libres me encanta jugar con el ordenador y mandar e-mails. También suelo hablar mucho por teléfono con mis amigos. Me gusta mucho montar en bici y nadar.

I am Marcelo. I am 14 years old. I live in Buenos Aires, in Argentina. We have a large family, 3 girls and 3 boys. That's a lot of children, isn't it? In my free time I love playing on the computer and sending e-mails. I also usually talk a lot to my friends on the telephone. I really like riding my bike and swimming.

Answers

(Corrections to false statements are shown in bold)

Gloria

1.	Gloria is Spanish.	True.
2.	She has an older sister.	False.
	Tiene una hermana menor.	**She has a younger sister.**
3.	She likes watching soap operas.	True.
4.	She is not very sporty.	False.
	Es muy deportista.	**She is very sporty.**

Alberto

5.	Alberto is Spanish.	False.
	Alberto es de Costa Rica.	**Alberto is from Costa Rica.**
6.	He has 3 sisters.	False.
	Tiene 2 hermanos.	**He has 2 brothers.**
7.	He likes playing the guitar.	True.
8.	On Sundays he goes to the disco.	False.
	Los sábados va a la discoteca.	**On Saturdays he goes to the disco.**

Raquel

9.	Raquel is from Madrid.	True.
10.	She works as a secretary.	False.
	Trabaja como profesora.	**She works as a teacher.**
11.	She likes going out with her friends on Saturdays and Sundays.	True.
12.	They have a good time.	True.

Marcelo

13.	Marcelo is Argentinian.	True.
14.	There are 9 people in his family.	False.
	Hay 8 personas en su familia.	**There are 8 people in his family.**
15.	In his free time he likes skiing.	False.
	En su tiempo libre le gusta jugar con el ordenador y mandar e-mails, hablar por teléfono, montar en bici y nadar.	**In his free time he likes computer and sending e-mails, talking on the telephone, riding his bike and swimming.**
16.	He really likes swimming.	True.

Those using the CD Rom can display the answers by clicking on the ? icons.

Immediate future
Pupil's Book: Page 147.

Pupils should have little trouble with this tense, which will allow them greatly to increase the range of ideas that they can express.

Ejemplos:

Voy a levantarme tarde	I am going to get up late.
Vas a levantarte a las 8	You are going to get up at 8.00.
Va a bañarse en la piscina	He is going to swim in the swimming pool.
Vamos a bañarnos en el mar	We are going to swim in the sea.
Vais a acostaros a las 10	You are going to go to bed at 10.00.
Van a acostarse temprano	They are going to go to bed early.

Exercise 6.35
Pupil's Book: Page 147.

1. Tomorrow I am going to write a letter to my friend.
2. Next Saturday you are going to go to a party, aren't you?
3. You are going to have a good time this weekend.
4. My mother is going to go shopping this morning.
5. We are going to see a film tonight.
6. You are going to ride your bike the day after tomorrow.
7. They are going to visit Spain next week.
8. You are going to learn Spanish.

Those using the CD Rom can display the translations by clicking on the Union Flag icons.

Exercise 6.36
Pupil's Book: Page 147.

1. *Esta tarde voy a hacer mis deberes.*
2. *Mañana va a jugar al baloncesto.*
3. *Vamos a ir de compras el sábado.*
4. *Van a ver un partido de fútbol.*
5. *¿Qué vas a hacer esta tarde?*
6. *Voy a ducharme.*
7. *¿Vais a acostaros?*
8. *Va usted a levantarse tarde?*

Those using the CD Rom can display the translations by clicking on the Spanish flag icons.

Exercise 6.37
Pupil's Book: Page 148.

In this exercise, pupils look at the eight pictures and reply to the question "What are you going to do tomorrow?" by dragging the appropriate infinitive into the gap (shown in bold). They can then translate.

1. *Voy a **escribir** (a mi abuela.)* — I am going to write (to my grandmother).
2. *Voy a **orar** (en la iglesia.)* — I am going to pray (in the church).
3. *Voy a **nadar** (en la piscina).* — I am going to swim (in the swimming pool).
4. *Voy a **ver** (la corrida.)* — I am going to watch (the bull fight).
5. *Voy a **bailar** (en la discoteca).* — I am going to dance (in the disco).
6. *Voy a **cenar** (en el restaurante).* — I am going to have dinner (in the restaurant).
7. *Voy a **estudiar** (en el colegio).* — I am going to study (in the school).
8. *Voy a **comprar** (las verduras).* — I am going to buy (the vegetables).

Those using the CD Rom can drag the correct infinitive onto the appropriate space.

Exercise 6.38
Pupil's Book: Page 148; Audio CD 2 tracks: 84-88

In this exercise, pupils listen to the five characters tell us what they normally do and what they are going to do now. The answers are then filled in on the table below.

Audio CD 2 Track 84:

1. *Yo soy Mónica. Normalmente me levanto a las 8 pero mañana voy a levantarme a las 10 porque es sábado y no tengo clase.*
   I am Mónica. Normally I get up at 8.00 but tomorrow I am going to get up at 10.00 because it is Saturday and I don't have any lessons.

Audio CD 2 Track 85:

2.   *¡Hola! Soy Mari-Carmen. Yo suelo hacer natación cada mañana pero hoy voy a montar en bici porque hace muy bueno.*
       Hello! I am Mari-Carmen. I usually go swimming every morning but today I am going to go bicycling because the weather is fine.

Audio CD 2 Track 86:

3.   *¡Hola, ¿qué tal? Me llamo Isabel. Normalmente voy al cine los sábados por la tarde con mis amigas pero este sábado voy al teatro con mis padres.*
       Hello! How is it going? My name is Isabel. Normally I go to the cinema with my friends on Saturday afternoons but this Saturday I am going to the theatre with my parents.

Audio CD 2 Track 87:

4.   *Yo me llamo Ana y mi amiga se llama Rosita. Normalmente tenemos clase de matemáticas los lunes, pero este lunes vamos a ver un video porque el profesor no está.*
       My name is Ana and my friend is called Rosita. We normally have a Maths class on Mondays, but this Monday we are going to watch a video because the teacher is away.

Audio CD 2 Track 88:

5.   *Te presento a Paloma, mi mejor amiga. Ella suele tocar la guitarra los viernes, pero esta semana va a bailar en la discoteca.*
       May I present Paloma to you, my best friend. She usually plays the guitar on Fridays but this week she is going to dance in the disco.

Answers:

Nombre	¿Qué hacen normalmente?	¿Qué van a hacer?
Mónica	se levanta a las 8	levantarse a las 10
Mari-Carmen	hace natación	montar en bici
Isabel	va al cine	ir al teatro
Ana y Rosita	tienen clase de matemáticas	ver un video
Paloma	toca la guitarra	bailar

Those using the CD Rom can display the answers by clicking on the ? icons.

Exercise 6.39
Pupil's Book: Page 148.

In this exercise, pupils practise the whole range of language that they have covered in the book by preparing and then conducting an interview with their partner. The suggested questions may be used as a prompt:

¿Qué vas a hacer esta tarde?	What are you going to do this afternoon?
¿Qué vas a hacer mañana?	What are you going to do tomorrow?
¿Qué vas a hacer este fin de semana?	What are you going to do this weekend?
¿Qué vas a hacer el sábado por la mañana?	What are you going to do on Saturday morning?
¿Qué vas a hacer en verano?	What are you going to do in the summer?
¿Qué vas a hacer en Navidad?	What are you going to do at Christmas?
¿Qué vas a hacer en Semana Santa?	What are you going to do in Holy Week (Easter)?
¿Qué vas a hacer durante las vacaciones?	What are you going to do during the holidays?